TITLE TOWN
USA

TITLE TOWN USA

Boxing in Upstate New York

Mark Allen Baker

Charleston   London

THE
History
PRESS

Published by The History Press
Charleston, SC 29403
www.historypress.net

Images are in the author's collection unless otherwise noted.

First published 2010

Manufactured in the United States

ISBN 978.1.59629.769.2

Library of Congress Cataloging-in-Publication Data

Baker, Mark Allen.
Title town, USA : boxing in Upstate New York / Mark Allen Baker.
p. cm.
Includes bibliographical references.
ISBN 978-1-59629-769-2
1. Boxing--New York (State)--Canastota--History. I. Title.
GV1125.B35 2010
796.830974764--dc22
2010011607

Notice: The information in this book is true and complete to the best of our knowledge. It is offered without guarantee on the part of the author or The History Press. The author and The History Press disclaim all liability in connection with the use of this book.

To family—

From the wonderful boxing genealogy of Upstate New York: the Basilios, Carmen, Joey and Billy Backus; the Brittons (Breslins), Jack and Bobby; the DeJohns (DiGiannis), Ralph, Carmen, Mike, Tommy, Lou, John and Joey; the Grahams (Geracis), Angelo "Bushy" Graham and Frankie Garcia; the Muscatos, Joe, Phil and Sam; the Pauls (Papas), Tommy, Al and Mickey; the Taylors, Joe and Johnny; the Tozzos, Joe "Kid" Kansas, Rocco "Rocky" Kansas and Tony Tozzo; and so many more.

To my own Upstate family: the Longs, the Latellas, the Wiskowskis, the Stapletons, the Allens and the Bakers.

UPSTATE NEW YORK

Famous Fight Series

—•—

Buffalo	Jack BRITTON v. Ted LEWIS
Syracuse, Buffalo	Sam LANGFORD v. Harry WILLS
Syracuse	Sam LANGFORD v. Sam McVEY
Syracuse	Sam LANGFORD v. Joe JEANNETTE
Albany	Sam LANGFORD v. Jim BARRY
Rochester	Battling LEVINSKY v. Jack DILLON
Albany	Joe LYNCH v. Jack SHARKEY
Syracuse	Charley WHITE v. Johnny DUNDEE
Buffalo	Harry GREB v. Jeff SMITH
Elmira	Jim BARRY v. Casper LEON
Buffalo	Jack BRITTON v. Johnny GRIFFITHS
Buffalo	Charley BURLEY v. Holman WILLIAMS

Contents

Foreword, by Edward Brophy   9

Acknowledgements   11

Introduction. Title Town, USA   13

1. Canastota, New York   21

2. Boxing in Upstate New York: The Fights   39

3. Boxing in Upstate New York: The People   61

4. Carmen Basilio: Road to Robinson   81

5. Billy Backus: Mission: "Mantequilla"   103

6. The International Boxing Hall of Fame   119

7. A Gallery of Champions   129

8. A Score to Settle: The Twentieth Anniversary   139

Selected Bibliography   155

About the Author   159

UPSTATE NEW YORK

Great Ring Battles

—◆—

Troy	March 31, 1891	George Dixon v. Cal McCarthy	KO22
Buffalo	July 3, 1899	George Kid Lavigne v. Frank Erne	L20
Buffalo	Jan. 15, 1900	Jim "Rube" Ferns v. Mys. Billy Smith	WF21
Buffalo	Feb. 8, 1912	Jack Dillon v. Paddy Lavin	ND10
Buffalo	Jan. 20, 1916	Jack Britton v. Ted Lewis	ND10
Buffalo	Dec.7, 1925	Rocky Kansas v. Jimmy Goodrich	W15
Buffalo	Feb. 10, 1930	Jimmy Slattery v. Lou Scozza	W15
Buffalo	June 25, 1930	Maxie Rosenbloom v. Jimmy Slattery	W15
Utica	Aug. 20, 1930	Bushy Graham v. Johnny Vacca	W10
Rochester	Nov. 11, 1938	Teddy Yarosz v. Ralph DeJohn	L10
Buffalo	Jan. 20, 1948	Phil Muscato v. Joe Matisi	W10
Syracuse	August 17, 1949	Joey DeJohn v. Lee Sala	KO by 6
Syracuse	Sept.18, 1953	Kid Gavilan v. Carmen Basilio	W15
Syracuse	Aug. 3, 1955	Tommy Jackson v. Ezzard Charles	W10
Syracuse	Sept.12, 1956	Carmen Basilio v. Johnny Saxton	KO9
Rochester	Oct. 26, 1979	Rocky Fratto v. Steve Michalerya	W10
Buffalo	June 1, 1984	Livingstone Bramble v. Ray Mancini	TKO14

Foreword

In 2009, the International Boxing Hall of Fame celebrated its landmark twentieth anniversary. This milestone provided a great opportunity to look back at twenty years of honoring the best in the sport while casting an eye toward the next twenty years. The mission of the hall—to honor and preserve boxing's rich heritage, chronicle the achievements of those who excelled and provide an educational experience for our many visitors—is vitally important to the "sweet science."

Since opening its doors to the public in 1989, the hall has strived daily to maintain its sacred mission through exciting exhibits of important boxing memorabilia from turn-of-the-century to modern stars. Authentic fight-worn items—including the gloves worn by George Dixon and Terry McGovern in a 1900 featherweight title bout, the boxing robe worn by Marvelous Marvin Hagler the night he won the middleweight championship and the trunks worn by Thomas Hearns when he won his fourth world title—are just some of the iconic pieces displayed. In 2007, the world-famous Madison Square Garden boxing ring was retired and donated to the hall for permanent display. Fans have the unique chance to stand "ringside" where Muhammad Ali and Joe Frazier met in the "Fight of the Century" on March 8, 1971.

The hall also houses one of the most complete research libraries on the sport of boxing. From newspaper clippings from the 1800s to the present and every issue of the *Ring*, boxing's history is saved here, and memories are kept alive. Boxing fans, media outlets and historians from around the world turn to the hall for answers. The hall also offers educational tours on the "sweet science," hosting groups of all ages eager to learn about boxing.

Left: An early photograph of the International Boxing Hall of Fame.

Below: Edward P. Brophy, executive director of the International Boxing Hall of Fame. *Courtesy IBHOF.*

The hall of fame is a way for Canastota to pay tribute to its two world champions—welterweight and middleweight champion Carmen Basilio and welterweight champion Billy Backus—and say thank you to the great sport that is woven into the fabric of the village. Canastota is "Boxing's Hometown" for the fistic legends and fans who love the sport.

Edward Brophy
Executive Director, International Boxing Hall of Fame

Acknowledgements

I would like to pass along my gratitude to The History Press, especially Whitney Tarella, Saunders Robinson, Jaime Muehl, Julie Foster and her production team, Dani McGrath, Amelia Lacey, Catherine Clegg, Lara Simpson, Brittain Phillips and, finally, Kate Pluhar.

I am extremely grateful to Edward P. Brophy, executive director of the International Boxing Hall of Fame, and his staff, especially Jeffrey S. Brophy, a ring scholar and consummate professional. Also to the IBHOF Board of Directors—Donald Ackerman, Bill LeMon, Darryl Hughto, Mike Milmoe, Paul Basilio, John Pantane, John Giamartino, Tony Vellano, Bob Davidson, Don Hamilton and Kathleen Rapasadi—and the chair people and volunteers, past and present, responsible for the annual IBHOF Induction Weekend. Finally, thank you to Tony Graziano, Billy Backus and Carmen Basilio.

I am also indebted to the following photographic resources: Canal Museum, Syracuse, New York; Canal Town Museum, 122 Canal Street, Canastota, New York—especially Joe DiGiorgio; HERITAGE AUCTIONS; the International Boxing Hall of Fame and its gifted photographer, Pat Orr (www.patorrphotography.com); Lelands' Sharon Mandell; and the Library of Congress and its outstanding staff. Also, I thank copyright barristers Herb Cohen and David Weinstein.

To my wonderful father-in-law, Richard Long, in my corner at the Lamb & Flag in London; to Aaron, Elizabeth and Rebecca, whom I will always second; and to my wife, Alison Long, with whom I share a ring—I am so very grateful.

Fabulous Fifties Fight Night

Syracuse, New York

War Memorial Auditorium

—◆—

July 31, 1952	Joey DEJOHN v. Henry Lee	KO 3
September 15, 1952	Joey DEJOHN v. Bob Murphy	KO 3
November 24, 1952	Ike WILLIAMS v. Pat Manzi	KO 7
August 28, 1954	Paddy YOUNG v. Joe Taylor	KO 10
April 1, 1955	Chico VEJAR v. Billy Graham	W 10
October 14, 1955	Tony BALDONI v. Ray Drake	W 10
April 12, 1957	Ralph "Tiger" JONES v. Chico Vejar	W 10
June 21, 1957	Rory Calhoun v. Joey Giambra	D 10
August 1, 1958	Yama BAHAMA v. Joe Miceli	W 10

Designed by Edgerton & Edgerton. Built from 1949 to 1951.
Selected entries. Caps=winner.

Introduction

Title Town, USA

"Title Town, USA," is a boxing moniker that belongs to Canastota, New York. It may have been claimed by others, but it hasn't been defended. It truly belongs to this Upstate hamlet.

Claiming powerful preeminence for any epicenter, the term actually connotes many things, beginning with a historic lineage. From the boys from Troy—John Morrissey and John C. Heenan—to New Paltz resident Floyd Patterson and Catskill's Mike Tyson, a championship course can be traced. The moniker then assumes that the very best must have fought in the area, not just in title fights but also in epic ring battles. It takes for granted that not only are the finest fighters produced here, but so are exceptional individuals in all aspects of the pastime. Equally important, it implies that the area professes a constant commitment to the "sweet science"—a distinctive undercurrent truly unique to the region. That's what the term means, and that is why it belongs to this township. But to be retained, the term must be explained and validated.

Boxing takes place in a ring, a confine restricted only by its footprint. The earliest champions—heavyweights—defended themselves in these Upstate New York arenas for a title that can be traced to this very day. But the very finest in the sport typically draw a large audience; therefore, when a legal match is made, it is typically held in an area that can comfortably accommodate demand. Centrally located in the state of New York, Canastota is less than 300 miles from Madison Square Garden, less than 150 miles from the Albany Convention Center and less than 25 miles from the War Memorial Auditorium in Syracuse, New York. It is, and has been,

Featherweight Willie Pep, a 1990 IBHOF inductee, was a frequent and beloved visitor to Canastota, New York.

accessible through modern transportation systems and is convenient to most fight fans, particularly those residing in Upstate New York.

This region has successfully drawn great fighters—a critical ingredient to our claim. They include some of the greatest fighters of all time, as determined by ring historians: Sugar Ray Robinson (Albany), Henry Armstrong (Buffalo), Willie Pep (Albany), Joe Louis (Buffalo), Harry Greb (Buffalo), Benny Leonard (Syracuse), Jack Dempsey (Buffalo), Mickey Walker (Binghamton), Tony Canzoneri (Utica), Joe Gans (Buffalo), Sam Langford (Syracuse), Stanley Ketchel (Albany), Ezzard Charles (Buffalo), Sugar Ray Leonard (Syracuse) and Barbados Joe Walcott (Utica). These ring giants have not only fought—be it prizefighting or exhibitions—in the cities listed inside the parentheses, but many have also battled throughout the area. The reason for this is simple: great fans. Preeminent fighters demand marquee fights in front of appreciative audiences, and Upstate New York has fulfilled that need with passionate pugilistic patrons, be they products of culture or simply lovers of the pastime.

Sam Langford, a 1990 IBHOF inductee, battled Harry Wills, Sam McVey, Joe Jeannette and Jim Barry in Upstate New York. *LC-DIG-ggbain-12254.*

Another attribute of a rich fisticuffs heritage is hosting epic ring battles. The area has accommodated a number of famous boxing campaigns—equally, if not more important than, title fights. They include: Jack Britton v. Ted Lewis (Buffalo), Sam Langford v. Harry Wills (Syracuse, Buffalo), Sam Langford v. Sam McVey (Syracuse), Sam Langford v. Joe Jeannette (Syracuse), Sam Langford v. Jim Barry (Albany), Battling Levinsky v. Jack Dillon (Rochester), Joe Lynch v. Jack Sharkey (Albany), Charley White v. Johnny Dundee (Syracuse), Harry Greb v. Jeff Smith (Buffalo), Jim Barry v. Casper Leon (Elmira), Charley Burley v. Holman Williams (Buffalo) and others. Undeniably, this is boxing at its finest!

A number of diverse title fights have also taken place in the region. Using Canastota's own Carmen Basilio as an example, the area witnessed his July 1953 USA New York State welterweight title fight against Billy Graham, his September 1953 world welterweight title fight against Kid Gavilan and his June 1955 world welterweight title fight against Tony DeMarco, all held at the War Memorial Auditorium in Syracuse, New York. Complimentary distinctions

Canastota's own Carmen Basilio, a 1990 IBHOF inductee, has been an inspiration to all of Upstate New York. *Courtesy IBHOF.*

can be important to our claim, such as "Fight of the Year," as acknowledged by reputable ring sources. They can also be title fights, like Basilio's world welterweight title battle against Johnny Saxton on September 12, 1956.

While hosting great fighters is paramount, an area must also produce its own. Upstate New York was home to boxers like Jimmy Slattery, Jimmy Goodrich, Tommy Paul, Steve Halaiko, Jack Sharkey, Bushy Graham, Nick Barone—and that is only the beginning. An adjunct to our affirmation is the production of outstanding fight families, including the Muscatos, the Tozzos, the Papas, the DiGiannis, the Basilios, the Brittons and the Geracis. Again, these are only a few names on a long list.

But Title Town is more than just fighters and fights. From cut men and trainers to matchmakers and managers, Upstate New York has provided the sport with a steady diet of ring talent, including individuals like William Muldoon, Roy Simmons Sr., Albert Wertheimer, Paul "Red" Carr, Jack Singer, Monsignor Franklin M. Kelliher, Jennie Grossinger, Norman Rothschild, Thomas A. Coulter, Ray Rinaldi, Rod Serling, Joyce Carol Oates, Pat Nappi, Billy Harris and many, many more. These are special men and women who have excelled in their vocation and contributed greatly to boxing.

In 1970, Billy Backus, Basilio's nephew, became the second Canastota resident to win a world title. *Courtesy IBHOF.*

Champions come in all shapes and sizes. From heavyweight champion of America John Morrissey to world middleweight champion Tommy Ryan, Upstate New York has produced some of boxing's finest. Some titleholders, like Carmen Basilio, have worn belts in multiple weight classes (welterweight and middleweight). The area has even produced related champions in the same weight class—for example, Billy Backus joined his uncle Carmen Basilio as world welterweight champion.

The International Boxing Hall of Fame would be enough to support the final ingredient for our designation, which is a constant commitment to the sport, but there is more. From the Buffalo Veteran Boxers Association–Ring #44 to the Rochester Boxing Hall of Fame, many communities have sought to acknowledge their own contributors within the sport. Digging ever deeper into their copious fisticuffs chronicle, these organizations complement one another by their very existence. They are further embellished by educational programs throughout the region that teach the art of self-defense in schools or in area clubs, forever proving the relevance of the activity.

Above: The traditional photograph session in front of the museum has become a fan favorite during Induction Weekend.

Left: The self-proclaimed "Greatest of All Time" Muhammad Ali in Canastota, New York. *Courtesy IBHOF*.

When a community not rich in per capita income but rich in heart turns out year after year in support of a mission, such as that of the World's Premier Boxing Institution, it is indeed something special and an event that should be acknowledged—a score and many more! In the eyes of village residents, you see undisputed endearment, affection for hard work, a sense of pride in ethnic heritage, love for one another and comfort in residence. This is their home.

So to every child prodigy on Peterboro or sparring hopeful along Hickory Street, look deep into the eyes of those who still remember the night Carmen defeated Ray for the middleweight crown or when "Our Billy" brought the belt back home and take pride in the fact that you live in Canastota, New York—"Title Town, USA."

POST–WORLD WAR II AREA BOXERS

Upstate New York—Outside Buffalo

* Al Jolson * Tony Forezzi * Billy Pinti * Aster Rice * Pete Virgin * Carmine Casale * Howie Brodt * Johnny DeNero * Len Taglia * Allen Faulkner * Tony Vero * Bill Franklyn * Vic Belanger * Pat Smith * Bill Foley * Allie George * Doug McDonald * Billy Carpenter * Joe Matisi * Eddie McGee * Frankie Best * Johnny Taylor * Jesse Jenkins * Johnny Kaufman * Nathan Brown * Joey Cardinal * Joey Kushner * Roosevelt Flagg * Hugo Bonacci * Tony DeMicco * Don Scaccia * Vern Roman * Johnny Rowe * Johnny Flynn * Nick Barone * Barney Taylor * Rolly Johns * Jimmy Evans * Ross Virgo * Frankie Basil * Jimmy Rouse * Leo West * Larry Bushing * Joey McPhee * Chet Vinci * Harry Smith * Eli Hall * Ernie Drummer * Jimmy DeMura * Jimmy Voss * Willie Bell * Johnny Pratt * Mike DeJohn * Jackie Donnelly * Al Simmons * Eddie Vick * Tony Ventura * Tommy Kost *

Assorted entries

THE MADISON SQUARE GARDEN RING

December 11, 1925	The First Fight: Paul Berlenbach v. Jack Delaney
August 27, 1943	Sugar Ray Robinson v. Henry Armstrong
October 26, 1951	Joe Louis v. Rocky Marciano (last MSG bout for both)
January 7, 1961	Carmen Basilio (last MSG bout) v. Gaspar Ortega
February 17, 1962	Sugar Ray Robinson (last MSG bout) v. Denny Moyer
July 17, 1964	Billy Backus (last MSG bout) v. Genaro Soto
March 8, 1971	The Fight of the Century: Muhammad Ali v. Joe Frazier
September 29, 1977	Muhammad Ali (last MSG bout) v. Earnie Shavers
June 13, 1986	Mike Tyson (last MSG bout) v. Reggie Gross
September 29, 2001	Bernard Hopkins defeats Felix Trinidad
June 9, 2007	The Final Fight: Miguel Cotto v. Zab Juddah

1

Canastota, New York

The geography of Upstate New York is as diverse as the people who would eventually inhabit it. The Native Americans, who were the first to learn how to survive and thrive on this land, built their villages nearby, and the area quickly became home. Subsequent inhabitants would also colonize and even modify the geography to fit their skills.

This land and the surrounding territory, over fifty-four thousand square miles, would eventually form the state of New York. Included among the state's geographic highlights are the Great Appalachian Valley, Lake Champlain, the Hudson River, the Adirondack Mountains, the Allegheny Plateau and the Catskill Mountains. The state also boasts the Allegheny River and rivers of the Susquehanna and Delaware systems, along with two Great Lakes—Erie and Ontario—which are connected by the Niagara River. Far from a cartographic challenge, nature's bounty creates three-quarters of a natural boundary, leaving man to define the state only to the south, with a simple horizontal line.

The Province of New York (1664–1775), a British colony, had borders similar to those of the present-day state. Progress was gradual, impeded often by the terrain, weather, finances and land disputes (if pugilism and colonization have something in common, it is claims). The area was the scene of much of the fighting in the French and Indian War, events that became familiar to most through depiction in the work of Cooperstown author James Fenimore Cooper.

Fighting with fists had been around for thousands of years. From ancient Ethiopia and Egypt to the Mediterranean region, a boxing-like sport spread.

Ancient Olympic programs included it, the Romans altered it and Christianity diffused it. However, a reemergence of the sport was inevitable and came in the late seventeenth century to Great Britain. Newspaper accounts acknowledged something like a combination of wrestling and boxing being conducted at the Royal Theatre in London. When it became clear that sustaining the sport meant refinement—and it didn't take long—options were considered. After opening a boxing academy in London in 1719, pugilist pioneer and first ring champion James Figg added a degree of skill to the sport when he combined it with his knowledge of fencing. Parries and ripostes soon became parrying and counterpunching as the sport gained an element of prestige.

The first recognized legal action taken by any governing body to ban professional boxing occurred in April 1743. An act of the British Parliament, initiated by an unsatisfactory bout between Jack Slack and James Broughton, prohibited this form of fighting by law in England. Broughton, the third recognized heavyweight champion of the prize ring, reigning from 1729 to 1750, would establish the first set of boxing rules and gloves in 1743.

THE ROAD TO FREEDOM

The sport of boxing was entrenched among the participants of the American Revolution. Amusement in New York, outside the battlefield, came at the expense of those chosen to fight private battles against British soldiers. It was nobleman and general Earl Percy (notable for his efforts at Concord), one of the commanders of British forces occupying the colony, who took "The Black Terror" Bill Richmond to England in 1777 to challenge all comers.

In Great Britain, the heavyweight title continued to change hands. From Slack, it went to Bill Stevens, then to George Meggs, Bill Darts, Tom Lyons, Ike Waterman, Harry Sellers, Harris Johnson, Tom Jackling, Big Ben Brain and Daniel Mendoza before John Jackson retired with it in 1795. In America, the first pugilistic encounter took place when Jacob Hyer defeated Tom Beasley in 1816. Hyer declared himself the bare-knuckle champion but never fought again; the title was vacant for twenty-five years.

Many of the settlers of Central and Western New York came from the New England states. The Central New York Military Tract, where Robert Harpur gave many of the townships the names of classical military and literary figures, was established to grant land to Revolutionary War veterans. These veterans found comfort in the land they had defended. Battles with the British were again fought here during the War of 1812.

The Canastota Canal Town Museum brings to life local folklore and history.

CANASTOTA, NEW YORK

Captain Reuben Parker purchased land, originally part of Oneida Indian Territory, and founded Canastota in 1810. The name was derived from the Oneida Indian word *Kniste-Stota*, which roughly translated means "cluster of pines near still or silent waters." Settlement began in customary fashion, first on what was expected to be the town's primary street, Main Street, followed by subsequent development outward. But the Industrial Revolution would alter plans eastward and onto Peterboro Street.

Like many centrally located New York State towns, Canastota prospered after the development of the Erie Canal, or the Great Western Canal, as it was also called. This waterway linked Buffalo on Lake Erie, part of the Great Lakes system, to Albany on the Hudson River; from Albany, it was 150 miles down the Hudson to the developed ports of New York City. Born from the prophecies of George Washington and the predictions of DeWitt Clinton, the waterway became a necessity after the War of 1812. It was this conflict that convinced many that the lack of adequate transportation facilities linking lands around Lake Erie and east could not only be dangerous

In 1810, Captain Reuben Perkins came to the area from New England and purchased 329.5 acres. *Courtesy Canastota Canal Town Museum.*

A view of Canal Street during the nineteenth century. *HABS NY, 27-CANA, 1-8.*

but tragic as well. Most of the roads were nothing more than old Indian trails—widened and packed down with dirt—that conformed to the seasons.

Construction began on the canal on July 4, 1817, under the leadership of New York State governor and primary canal advocate Dewitt Clinton. The 363-mile canal, with eighty-three locks and eighteen aqueducts, would be hailed as the greatest engineering accomplishment of its time. It would be divided into three sections: a downward-sloping western segment running 165 miles from Lake Erie to the Seneca River, a middle section of flat landscape covering 72 miles from the Seneca River to Rome at the headwaters of the Mohawk River and, finally, a steep slope of over 126 miles from Rome to Albany on the Hudson. The proposed dimensions of the canal were forty feet wide on the surface tapered to twenty-eight feet wide on the bottom at a depth of four feet.

The idea of a waterway transportation system was not new; it had been employed successfully in Europe with tremendous efficiency. However, the longest canal in North America up to this point was a twenty-seven-mile waterway built in the 1700s, linking Boston to the Merrimack River. This new task, however, was an enormous undertaking presenting an entirely new set of challenges. The question most often asked was why.

A canal system was attractive because it did not have to deal with river currents. A calm surface was more conducive to safe and reliable transportation. Also, significantly more freight could be moved at no slower a pace than that of a horse-drawn wagon over a road. As the boats would have no motive of power, they would be pulled by beasts of burden—horses or mules—walking along a towpath by the side of the canal. An operator, either walking or riding on a horse, could work in conjunction with a man steering the boat.

Local pride ran deep; thus, townsfolk were employed over contractors for digging—a quality assurance, as well as recruitment, guarantee. Villages and cities flourished once the project began, and when the canal opened, living standards and wages improved. The growth in manufacturing and improvements in labor productivity would be astounding.

Since the middle section of the three-part canal plan was the easiest to build, it would begin first. A portion of that segment was called the Long Level, a stretch of fifty-nine miles of very flat land from Utica to Syracuse. This stretch, which included Canastota, would become the longest canal level in the world that did not include a lock.

The most significant challenge the canal route faced was encountered from Rochester to Lake Erie. A section of formidable cliffs needed to be conquered. Since this route was the only way to guarantee adequate water supply, there were no alternatives. After several engineers submitted proposals to the canal commission, a solution was chosen. Nathan Roberts, a resident of Canastota and an engineer (chief on the stretch of canal between Rome and Syracuse), conceived a flight of locks to climb sixty feet up the embankment. It would become the most breathtaking experience along the entire route.

The city of Syracuse—eventually the closest major metropolitan area to Canastota—was originally only a couple of homes and a tavern. In 1825, the same year the canal opened, it incorporated as a village. The combination of the Erie Canal and the rich salt deposits—for which the area had been known since the 1700s—would industrialize the region. The "salt and water" recipe saw the population of Syracuse escalate.

The first *official* boat on the canal left Buffalo on October 26, 1825, and reached New York City nine days later, on November 4. It passed through sixteen counties, from Albany County to the east to Erie County to the west. The $7 million enterprise cut travel time by one-third and shipping cost by

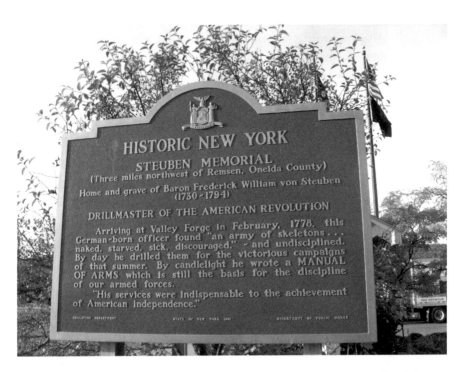

This Historic New York signs document the role of the state during the American Revolution.

nine-tenths and opened up the Great Lakes area. The boats were typically manned by a steward, two helmsmen, two drivers and a captain. Since the canal froze in the winter, all travel came to a halt. This meant that some boat crews found residence in towns along the waterway until spring.

Perhaps the most famous person to venture down the canal prior to its official opening was the last surviving general of our War of Independence, the Marquis de Lafayette, who boarded a canalboat in Lockport for passage to Rochester and Syracuse before arriving in Utica on June 8, 1825. Naturally, many passengers would follow as word of this miraculous achievement spread worldwide.

A consistent flow of new visitors meant additional commerce for all of the canal towns, including Canastota. The site of only four homes in 1817, Canastota established a post office in 1829 and had three public houses, three stores and a population of 406 by 1831. In 1835, the village was officially incorporated. By 1839, additional commerce had necessitated the widening of the canal and had even attracted the railroad. Both bolstered employment options and land values.

Boxing, too, was thriving, and as we will note later, it was also a benefactor of the canal. By 1841, Jacob Hyer's son, Tom, had claimed his father's title. This was challenged in New York City—unsuccessfully—by George McChaster, or "Country McCloskey," who found the younger Hyer a well-suited and puissant champion. Hyer then met English battler Yankee Sullivan, who was in the United States, on February 7, 1849, at Stillpond Creek, Maryland. All skeptics were quickly put to rest when Hyer knocked out his opponent in the sixteenth round. So convincing was the American's skills that he could no longer find any challengers, so he retired.

JOHN C. MORRISSEY

John C. Morrissey was born in Templemore, County Tipperary, Ireland, in 1831. Two years later, his parents immigrated to the United States and settled in Troy, New York. Not happy with what he saw as his future, the young and troubled adolescent left Troy for New York City. There he fell into the gangs, earning a fierce reputation as a battler and the nickname "Old Smoke." The moniker was acquired during a fight with a gang member named Tom McCann. Morrissey, who was pinned on his back atop burning coals from an overturned stove, endured tremendous pain but fought off his opponent. He regained his feet and beat McCann senseless.

John Morrissey (1831–1878) was a fighter, bare-knuckle boxer, state senator and U.S. congressman. *LC-DIG-cwpbh-04834.*

After two years in New York, Morrissey headed west, like some, seeking fame and fortune during the California Gold Rush but also in pursuit of heavyweight champion Tom Hyer. What he couldn't find in the mines, he quickly found on a card table. Morrissey became a renowned gambler. It was also during this time that he appeared for the first time in a professional prizefighting ring. Morrissey knocked out George Thompson on August 31, 1852. This success encouraged him to return to New York, still in pursuit of Hyer but willing to tackle the popular cognoscente Yankee Sullivan.

After repeated taunting, Sullivan acquiesced to Morrissey on October 12, 1853. As boxing was illegal in most places during the 1850s, the prohibited match took place in the mountainous terrain of the hard-to-find village of Boston Corners, New York. Those who were able to witness the contest saw thirty-seven tough rounds of a Sullivan defeat. Irishman Morrissey, a hero in local eyes, gained national renown with his victory. Five years later, he would also defeat Troy native John C. Heenan before retiring from the ring.

Influential in the development of Saratoga Springs, New York, Morrissey then turned to Washington, D.C., and the floor of the House of Representatives (1867–71)—a battle of different sorts, but no less challenging. He served in the New York State Senate beginning in 1875 until his death in 1878.

THE MUCKLANDS

A vast swamp north of the village of Canastota was cleared to reveal a rich black earth called "muck." It was fertile soil, abundant in nutrients, composed of glacial deposit—phosphorus combined with concentrations of plant matter. If made workable, it could satisfy the dreams of many area farmers. Early attempts to drain these wetlands had proven moderately successful, cost-effective and efficacious. As funds became available, drainage ditches were enlarged, eventually leading to the construction of an artery through the wild area—the so-called Oniontown Road. As hundreds of acres of rich farmland became available, the older farming residents of Canastota needed to hire labor—hardworking people they could depend on—so they turned to their neighbors, mostly Italian immigrants. Accustomed to the overworked farmland in southern Italy, they were the perfect solution.

Working the mucklands for the owner of the property, these sharecroppers or tenant farmers traditionally received seeds, tools and other necessities from the landlord. These perks could also include housing—a tempting offer. Paid a percentage from the harvested crop, the goal for many was to save enough money for a down payment on their own land or farm and an opportunity to mimic the process. It was a family affair that transpired seven days a week, rain or shine, with only time off for Sunday Mass. It was an arduous and volatile environment. A bad storm could mean the loss of crops, months of hard work and many dreams.

Shanties or homes were built along the roads leading through the mucklands. From early April until harvesting was complete—around October—this area became home. Familiar voices rising in customary song or the smell of a common recipe emulating from a wood-burning stove became cherished memories for many. As a neighbor fondly recalls, "The shanties were kept immaculate, and considering how the slightest breeze could fill it with muck, this was not an easy task. Depending upon the time of year that Pasqua [Easter] fell on, you might catch the aroma of traditional Easter bread filling the air."

Thanks to the early immigrants, Canastota grew into the onion capital of the United States by the 1920s and 1930s. While the major crops were edible bulbs, other vegetables—such as lettuce, celery and carrots—were also bountiful. "We knew who owned the one-, two-, five- or ten-acre sections," a resident recalls. "As we drove down Warner Road, which ran past Route 13—north of the village—to Pine Ridge Road we could name the names, like Lumbrazo, Nastasi, Cesarini…We knew them all."

The Railroad

The railroad also became a propitious employment option for residents. At the turn of the twentieth century, "section gangs" were employed and responsible for track maintenance in the area. To move with celerity, road crew foremen often turned to the hardest-working people they knew—their neighbors. Difficult work, especially during the winter months when track rails cracked like glass, was augmented by limited communication. There were no phones. Word of mouth, in a variety of languages, would spread the news that there was a break and a crew was needed. The canal had even spawned the first steam railroad in the United States, the Mohawk & Albany, which opened for business in 1831 between Albany and Schenectady. Others soon followed.

By the late 1960s, the rail system was changing, and the New York Central System merged with Penn Central. Transportation was evolving, and nobody knew that better than Canastota residents. Many of their families had witnessed the evolution of the Erie Canal system. When Penn Central headed toward bankruptcy in 1971, it seemed that the writing was on the wall for many residents. Numerous bankrupt railroads finally joined with Conrail in 1976, including Penn Central, but this meant more changes. During the era, grade crossings were also eliminated—from Beebee Bridge to east of Oneida—as was the train station, now replaced by an overpass.

Boxing Along the Erie Canal

Immigrants, including large numbers of Irish, worked on or along the canal. It was a transient lifestyle not surprisingly influenced by maritime culture. These iron-muscled bargemen were known to frequent local saloons at stops along the canal. Wagering a pint or two over a bare-knuckled brawl became acceptable behavior as canallers, or canawlers, developed their own culture. After colonial times, and before the railways, the behavior, music, folklore and language of canallers filled a cultural vacuum. It also migrated into the cultures found along the canal.

Exchanging boxing stories was also commonplace along canal stops, and news traveled fast when any of them involved a local pugilist. Such was the case during the 1870s, when a handsome Irish gentleman dubbed "The Trojan Giant" emerged on the scene. Born in the town of Thurles, County Tipperary, Ireland, Paddy Ryan eventually found his way to Troy, New York.

CHAMPION PUGILISTS OF THE WORLD.
Presented by the LISTON BEEF COMPANY of Chicago. Ills.
N.Y. OFFICE, 113 WEST BROADWAY.

Champion Pugilists of the World featuring Paddy Ryan, 1885. *LC-DIG-pga-00188.*

On May 30, 1880, he won the American heavyweight title by defeating Joe Goss in eighty-seven rounds at Collier's Station, West Virginia. Years later, Ryan would lose his title to a different Sullivan, rising star John L. Sullivan, now recognized as the first heavyweight champion of gloved boxing. Sullivan is also generally recognized as the last heavyweight champion of bare-knuckle boxing under the London Prize Ring rules and the first American sports hero to become a national celebrity. Ryan would later settle in Watervliet, New York (north of Albany), and recall fondly battling along the Erie Canal.

On September 8, 1894, the first motion picture camera filming of a fight was accomplished through the use of Thomas Edison's Kinescope at the Edison Laboratory in Orange, New Jersey. Although this feat had been fairly acknowledged and well documented, a similar technical achievement was not. The first motion picture projection was shown in November 1895 at the rear of a building located on West Center Street in Canastota. Coincidentally, the subject of the film was a boxing bout.

Milton De Lano (August 11, 1844–January 2, 1922) was a United States representative from New York. Born in Wampsville, he settled in Canastota.

The photographic process used was known as the Biograph, and its inventor, W.K.L. Dickson, was a frequent visitor to Canastota. On August 5, 1895, while still perfecting his creation, Dickson used his invention to record a sparring match between Professor A.I. Leonard and his pupil, Bert Hosley. The first projected fight film was finally shown to a small gathering outside Mahan's Machine Shop. A makeshift screen was set up outside the building, while the projector remained inside the shop with the lens pointing through the window. Triumphant in his success, Dickson loaded up his impressive invention and took it to a theatre in New York City.

By the turn of the century, the village was taking shape, developing a character of its own and attracting its own cultural mix. Mimicking similar towns of its size, particularly those along the canal, its commerce reflected the needs of the people. Government grew, attracting many distinguished public servants such as Thomas Barlow, and services, including a fire company and police department, took shape. Businesses found a home, the Watsons brought their wagons to Canastota and the Lee Manufacturing Company was attracting new employees. A library was even established in the old Perkins home, later the White Elephant.

Equally as dynamic as the growth of a prosperous village was the heavyweight division, which dominated the sport and reflected the changing times. Gentlemen Jim Corbett picked up where Sullivan left off, followed by Robert Fitzsimmons, now an American citizen. James J. Jeffries would retire as champion, at least for the first time, passing the title to Marvin Hart, who beat Jack Root. From Tommy Burns, the title went to the controversial Jack Johnson. "The Galveston Giant" reflected the turmoil in society that led to the "Fight of the Century" between himself and the retired James J. Jeffries. From champion Johnson—the title was also claimed by Sam Langford, who didn't press the issue—the title went to Jess Willard, who lost it to Jack Dempsey. Gene Tunney defeated Dempsey twice and then retired as an undefeated heavyweight after his victory over Tom Heeney in 1928.

When Binghamton-born Jack Sharkey knocked out the former light heavyweight champion Tommy Loughran to win the United States heavyweight title, Upstate New York established another heavyweight boxing link. His 1929 Yankee Stadium victory earned him the opportunity to fight for the vacant world title against the German contender, Max Schmeling. Sharkey was disqualified, however, in the fourth round during the June 12, 1930 fight.

During the early twentieth century, much of Canastota's pugilistic exploits centered on the Canastota High School boxing teams and the American Legion, a practice that was not uncommon, as not only was boxing taught in school, but it was also encouraged by other institutions. The most exciting boxer at the time was a scrappy fighter named Jimmy DeCapua. The transplanted boxer and former state of Michigan welterweight champion fought Mike McTigue in 1929. McTigue, one of the best "no-decision" fighters of his era, had beaten Battling Siki for the world light heavyweight championship in 1923. By the time he fought DeCapua, McTigue was at the end of a great career, and Jimmy was struggling with a not-so-pretty variation. DeCapua's last documented Upstate New York appearance was against Troy's Larry Marinucci at the arena in Syracuse.

The first part of the twentieth century also saw great waves of European immigration. Their children, the next generation, hadn't succeeded yet in business, politics or academics and were looking for alternatives. It was sports, such as boxing, that offered them a chance for glory and a glimpse of fame. Boxing was rooted in the culture of the country and celebrated in many forms. When a poor boy dreamed of escaping his formidable life, his fantasy was often of fighting his way out as a boxer and becoming a professional athlete.

This was the embodiment of America's melting pot theory. The fairness of society was reflected in its preeminent athletes. The fact that three sons of an immigrant fisherman named DiMaggio could play Major League Baseball or a trio of Buffalo boys named Tozzo could box became incentive to many. European immigrants were quick to find comfort in the neighborhoods of Upstate New York, especially in the cities and towns that adorned the Erie Canal. For example, when the canal was finished, many of the Irish settled west of Syracuse on a hill overlooking Clinton's Ditch. This area became known as Tipperary Hill, as it was settled primarily by Irish immigrants, many of whom hailed from County Tipperary. To say that ethnic pride runs deep in the region is perhaps an understatement, best proven by the fact that the only traffic light in the country where the Irish green is above British red still exists on Tipperary Hill.

Pride also came from local residents willing to share their knowledge of the sport they loved. Boxing was always paramount to Canastota resident Eddie Gordie. He was quick to impress the neighborhood youth with his boxing stances and willingness to teach self-defense.

The 1940s would find Canastota native Ben Sgroi helping to carry the Syracuse University boxing team to the intercollegiate boxing championship. Sgroi, along with Sam Giufre, was just one of the many standouts from the local boxing team. The next two decades, however, would find the entire town living vicariously through the efforts of a boxer named Basilio.

No stranger to how towns can benefit from improved transportation systems, Canastota residents witnessed an immediate impact following the opening, in 1954, of the New York State Thruway. Once again, the warmth of a small village became a residential option from all directions. Residents were also taking advantage of the many Syracuse employment opportunities resting just off the major transportation arteries, including the General Electric Corporation, the Carrier Corporation and General Motors.

The prosperous 1950s were also ripe for entrepreneurship, as new businesses took root in the village. Perhaps the most often recalled example is Dominic Bruno's purchase of the building at 112 Center Street and its transformation into the White Elephant. Taking a page out of the Georgetown Inn's playbook, Bruno booked well-known entertainers at the establishment. To hear the sounds of "Racing with the Moon," "In the Still of the Night" or "Let It Snow, Let It Snow, Let It Snow" as Vaughn Monroe serenaded the town was quite a treat for local residents. Bruno would also go on to work his magic at the Three Rivers Inn in Phoenix, where he hosted many popular entertainers.

Dickie DiVeronica, born on January 26, 1938, ranked as high as eighth in the world and was the next Canastota clouter to lace 'em up. One of four boys—Anthony, John, Rocco and Ricardo ("Dickie")—born to Paul and Julia DiVeronica, he was a proficient and solid welterweight at five feet, six inches tall. Turning professional in 1958, he quickly shot to an impressive 18-0 record. His first loss—far from an embarrassment—came at the hands of an undefeated Buffalo lightweight, Jackie Donnelly, in his hometown. He then won his next two battles, including a decision over Utah's Jay Fullmer, before losing a Donnelly rematch. His boxing career came to an abrupt end with a call from Uncle Sam; he was drafted into the United States Army in August 1961.

Honorably discharged in the fall of 1963, he turned again toward the ring, defeating Pete Toro and Les Bagi. A fervid DiVeronica even found himself back inside Madison Square Garden, for the fifth time in his career; he defeated Tommy Garrison. Finding it harder and harder to find matches locally, his managers—Joe Netro and Johnny DeJohn, both of Basilio fame—sent him to Miami to work with Angelo Dundee and Izzy Klein at the famous Fifth Street Gym. There he sharpened his skills, even working

Canastota's own Dickie DiVeronica, a welterweight contender, fought many of the finest in his day, including Emile Griffith. *Courtesy IBHOF.*

with future hall of fame boxer Luis Rodriguez. As he improved as a fighter, so did his opponents, who included Savannah's Gordon Lott and New Orleans's Percy Pugh.

Every good fighter has a classic fight series, and DiVeronica was no exception. His 1967 Baltimore trilogy against D.C.'s Herbie Lee was an outstanding twenty-six-round confrontation. On April 3, Lee, a confident local favorite, entered the ring with only one loss. In front of a stunned crowd of fewer than two thousand, DiVeronica dropped him to the canvas in a sixth-round knockout. Humiliated, Lee immediately called for a rematch, which was promptly scheduled for May 25. The Civic Center crowd then watched as Lee danced ten rounds to a split decision. By now, an incensed and ineluctable DiVeronica had had enough; their final July 10 battle belonged to him. Dickie took two out of three from "Sweet" Herbie Lee.

On July 11, 1969, DiVeronica entered the ring at the War Memorial Auditorium in Syracuse against future hall of fame member Emile Griffith—a confirmation of his skills. The valiant effort ended in a seventh-round TKO loss to Griffith. It was heartfelt to his fans and marked his final Upstate New York appearance. Finishing his professional career at a respectable 42-13-1, "Dickie D." hung up the gloves in 1972. Since that time, he has been one of the hall of fame's greatest advocates and remains a bona fide fan favorite each Induction Weekend. DiVeronica passed the Canastota torch to another welterweight contender named Howard William "Billy" Backus, the nephew of Carmen Basilio, who won the world welterweight title on December 3, 1970.

Upstate New York also saw another heavyweight champion, albeit an adopted one, in the person of Floyd Patterson, from Waco, North Carolina. Patterson, who would reside in both Rockville Centre and, later, in New Paltz, New York, had command of the heavyweight ranks from November 1956 until September 1962, minus a brief interlude to Ingemar Johansson. After Patterson, Upstate New York would have hooks in the heavyweight title through associated individuals. For example, Angelo Dundee, who worked with Carmen Basilio, also trained Cassius Clay (Muhammad Ali), who held the belt throughout most of the remainder of the decade.

The original Canastota Boxing Club was formed in the early 1960s and headed by a trio of ring enthusiasts: Ernest Emmi and Joe DeMauro of Canastota, along with Tony Rinaldo of Oneida. For nearly two decades, they promoted professional boxing in Central New York—Syracuse, Utica, Binghamton, Rochester and even Alexandria Bay. They became an integral part of the boxing fabric that has given their town such great distinction.

Graziano's Casa Mia, operated by Tony Graziano, has become a must-visit for every boxing fan.

Showcased local talent included Hal "TNT" Carroll of Syracuse, Dickie DiVeronica and, later, Rocky Fratto of Geneva.

Born in Utica, New York, Tony Graziano was no stranger to confrontation or the "sweet science." His D-day participation as a paratrooper during World War II alone would be enough to impress most, but so would his early boxing days in West Palm Beach, running boxers into Cuba three times a week. Eventually returning to Upstate New York and Canastota, he set up a gym in town and began nurturing and even promoting the talent around him. You see, Graziano has a knack for spotting potential and the aptitude to enhance it. He's a pugilistic paragon. Instrumental in guiding Billy Backus to the world welterweight crown and managing many fighters, including Rocky Fratto, a North American junior middleweight champion, Graziano, too, has been a gift to boxing. Today, you can find the legendary trainer at his restaurant, Graziano's Casa Mia, which transforms into a who's who of boxing during Induction Weekend.

It is during this very special weekend in June that Graziano's Casa Mia becomes the Toots Shorr's of Madison County. Everywhere you look, there is someone special affiliated with the sport. One story I witnessed and have often recounted involves a couple from out of town who entered the restaurant and asked the waitress for directions and a takeout menu. As they departed, I heard the gentleman tell his wife, "You know, we ought to come back here later. The waitress told me some of the boxers come here. Some of the very best to have ever entered the ring." While exiting, the couple passed a seating section without giving it so much as a glance. Spinning ring tales at the table were Tony Graziano, Beau Jack, Archie Moore and historian Hank Kaplan.

The end of the last century saw boxing's heavyweight division dominated by a single name, Michael Gerard Tyson. Born in Brooklyn, Tyson lived in Bedford-Stuyvesant and Johnstown before ending up in Catskill, New York—just over 150 miles from Canastota—under the watchful eye of Cus D'Amato. Tyson would become the undisputed heavyweight champion and the youngest man ever to win the WBC, WBA and IBF world heavyweight titles. He won the WBC title at just twenty years, four months and twenty-two days old. Forever controversial, and clearly one of the greatest heavyweights of all time, "Iron Mike" is also destined for Canastota.

What an honor the moniker "Title Town, USA," has been for everyone in Canastota, not only for those who live in and around this historic village but also for the thousands who visit annually. For over two decades, they have witnessed a town in transition, a village in a state of rediscovery. Worthy of the International Boxing Hall of Fame and exemplary of a sport woven into the fabric of American history, "Title Town" is the perfect encomium. But similar to the ruby slipper–wearing Dorothy Gale, whose epiphany at the end of *The Wizard of Oz* became so obvious, wasn't the answer always here to begin with? When you put all the pieces together, as you will by reading this book, all of the historic evidence supports this claim: Upstate New York, with Canastota at its epicenter, really is boxing's Mecca.

2

Boxing in Upstate New York

The Fights

With Canastota as its cornerstone, Upstate New York is steeped in boxing tradition. From early pugilistic accounts of British occupants to laborers' tales along the banks of the Erie Canal, the region exudes every fascinating element of the "sweet science." Beneath the marquee of "Title Town, USA," are six simple words: "The very best have fought here."

"Upstate" and "Downstate" are frequent terms used to distinguish between New York State counties north of suburban Westchester and Rockland Counties on the one hand and the New York City metropolitan area on the other. Outstanding fighters in all weight classes trained and fought in nearly every major city in Upstate New York. They traveled by horseback, carriage, boat, rail car and even airplane to arrive at their destinations. Not all fights were acknowledged or recorded, but boxing was commonplace.

To ensure its safety or control, rules and regulations—governed by a country, state or organization—eventually caught up with boxing. These rules, some written and others merely tolerated, prohibited fighters from boxing without a license or fighting at certain venues and even prevented fighters from certain ethnicities from battling one another. The Frawley Act, passed in 1911, was an attempt to stop fixed fights. Thus was born the "No Decision" era, which took place from about 1911 to 1920. The concept was that a fix was less likely if the only way to win was a knockout. Of course, fight fans are binary and demand a winner, so the media took it upon themselves to declare their own decisions, commonly called "newspaper decisions." The Walker Law of 1920 put an end to this era.

Johnny Kilbane, a 1995 IBHOF inductee, fought in numerous cities in Upstate New York. *LC-DIG-ggbain-10281.*

Some boxers fought under assumed names to avoid detection, legal or prejudicial, or even used the names of former ring greats to intimidate opponents. It also became common for fighters to use a variety of names or monikers; for example, Louis D'Ambrosio used the ring name Lou Ambers and the nickname "Herkimer Hurricane." If you add to this venues that also changed names and locations, you have a record-keeping nightmare.

Fight records, especially those kept during our nation's infancy, are incomplete. Even to this day, historians are discovering ring battles from the past. During my years preparing press kits for the International Boxing Hall of Fame, boxing historian Hank Kaplan would often contact us with modified ring records based on his comprehensive research. Many sources, while vigilantly addressing this problem, conflict with one another regarding fight accounts on details like dates, opponents, weights, records, venues, cities, fight lengths and decisions.

Then there is the issue of weight class. In the days when Carmen Basilio was taking on all comers, there were only eight (there are currently seventeen) weight divisions: flyweights (112 pounds), the smallest fighters; bantamweights (118 pounds); featherweights (126 pounds); lightweights (135 pounds); welterweights (147 pounds); middleweights (160 pounds); light heavyweights (175 pounds); and finally, heavyweights (190 pounds or more). For aggressive fighters, this meant that weight adjustments were in order to fight for multiple titles—not a simple task!

Keeping all of these elements in mind, we begin our pugilistic review, or tour if you will, of Upstate New York. Not every boxer is mentioned, nor is every great fight, but the list should create a flood of memories for every boxing fan and certainly support our "Title Town, USA," premise. The cities are listed alphabetically and begin, in most cases, with the heavyweights.

ALBANY AND SURROUNDING AREA (SCHENECTADY, TROY)

The state capital area, about 125 miles from Canastota, has witnessed many hall of fame boxers, including Battling Battalino, Jack Britton, Panama Al Brown, Kid Chocolate, Young Corbett II, Dixie Kid (Aaron Brown), George Dixon, Frankie Genaro, Pete Herman, Stanley Ketchel, Battling Levinsky, Ted (Kid) Lewis, Joe Lynch, Willie Pep, Sandy Saddler, Joe Walcott (Barbados) and Mickey Walker. Other notable fighters include Melio Bettina, George Chip, Leach Cross, Harry Forbes, Abe Goldstein, Bushy Graham, Bill Hurley, Johnny Jadick, Mike McTigue, Bob Olin, Ken Overlin, Eddie "Babe" Risko and Marty Servo.

But modern heavyweight history belongs to one of the most feared and controversial boxers in the history of the sport—Michael Gerard Tyson of Brooklyn, New York. He began his rise under the tutelage of legendary trainer Constantine "Cus" D'Amato. Eventually becoming Tyson's legal guardian and personal mentor, D'Amato molded and perfected his fighter into a modern-day heavyweight legend. "Iron" Mike, standing five feet, ten inches tall (in an orthodox stance) with limited reach, found Marciano's trademarked center of gravity and leveraged it beyond comprehension. While compiling an impressive 24-3 amateur record in numerous events, including the national Golden Gloves and the 1984 U.S. Olympic trials, he was schooled in the sport's rich history by D'Amato, who is credited with his early success.

Tyson's pro debut took place at the Plaza Convention Center in Albany against Hector Mercedes. His adversary, who would win only one fight in his entire career, was a Mercedes only in name. In a prelude to what would become his early hallmark, Tyson knocked out his opponent in the first round. Tyson's subsequent area victims included Chicago's Trent Singleton (1985-TKO1); Lowell's Don Halpin (1985-KO4); Cleveland's Larry Sims (Mid-Hudson Civic Center, Poughkeepsie, 1985-KO3); Trinidad's Sterling Benjamin (Latham Coliseum, Latham, 1985-TKO1); Canadian Conroy Nelson (Latham Coliseum, Latham, 1985-TKO2); Charlotte's Mark Young (Latham Coliseum, Latham, 1985-TKO1) and Toledo's tall David Jaco (Plaza Convention Center, Albany, 1986-TKO1).

In 1986, Tyson tackled Jesse Ferguson at Rensselaer Polytechnic Institute in Troy. It would be the longest fight victory to date—a six-round TKO—for the Catskill fighter who would tame the Philly Thunder. Ferguson, while down in the fifth round, was disqualified for excessive holding, a common technique utilized by an overmatched or tired fighter. Later that same year, another Tyson victim, Chicago's William Hosea, hit the canvas before his corner pulled the stool (1986-KO1).

The Civic Center in Glen Falls also hosted a couple of Tyson battles, including Tulsa's James "Quick" Tillis (1986-W10) and Philadelphia's Marvis Frazier (1986-KO1). Although Tillis went down in the fourth round, he managed to stay the distance; he was the first Tyson opponent to do so. Referee Joe Cortez called out Frazier at the thirty-second mark of the first round. Tyson, who would never fight in New York State again, ended his Empire State career 17-0, with all but one fight ending in some form of knockout.

The Upstate New York middleweight division can be traced back to hall of fame member Mike Donovan. The Chicago-born battler fought Dick Liston, in Troy, New York, under prize ring rules, with gloves, for five rounds back in March 1877. A gifted instructor, Donovan fought out of New York City and was a ring favorite at Harry Hills, the legendary fight venue.

The talented "Sugar" Ray Robinson knocked out Schenectady's Vinny Vines (1946-KO6) at Hawkins Stadium in Albany. Vincenzo Semprevino (aka Vinny Vines) fought until 1948 and was familiar to Upstate boxing fans through battles at the LaSalle Gym in Troy or perhaps the Kalurah Temple in Binghamton. He fought some good fighters in his day, including Izzy Jannazzo, Fritzie Zivic, Cocoa Kid and Holman Williams.

Emile Griffith fought twice in the Albany area. He first picked up a win in 1963 against Holly Mims, who was at the end of his career, at a bout held in

Featherweight Abe Attell, a 1990 IBHOF inductee, was a fluid boxer with excellent defensive skills. *LC-DIG-ggbain-08235.*

Saratoga Springs. Griffith would later return a dozen years later, at the end of his run, and fight to a victory over Jose Chirino.

World featherweight champion Abe Attell knocked out Harry Forbes (1910-KO7) in a vicious Troy battle of note. Forbes went down four times! Attell, a gifted hall of fame fighter, is forever linked to the infamous Black Sox baseball scandal of 1919. An alleged accomplice to gambler Arnold Rothstein, the San Francisco–born fighter supposedly gave $10,000 to several Chicago White Sox players. The "Black Sox," as they would be known, had, in return, agreed to throw the World Series with Cincinnati. When the scandal broke in 1920, Attell went to Canada for a year to avoid being subpoenaed. He would later find solace in the small Upstate New York town of New Paltz, as would boxer Floyd Patterson.

The great Stanley Ketchel kayoed Tony Caponi in Schenectady back in 1909 (KO4). "The Michigan Assassin" was unstoppable during this period of his career, until he decided to step up against Jack Johnson about four months later. In the twelfth round, Johnson dropped Ketchel to the canvas for only the second time in his career.

BINGHAMTON

The only boxer to fight both Jack Dempsey and Joe Louis hails from Binghamton; he was Joseph Paul Cukoschay, or Jack Sharkey. Born in 1902, Sharkey fought primarily out of Boston, Massachusetts. Ironically, he earned the respect of many through a ring loss to the popular and gifted Jack Dempsey in 1927. Sharkey's performance was so spectacular that it nearly earned him a fight with Gene Tunney. Sharkey would later lose a bid for the vacant world heavyweight title by a fourth-round foul against Max Schmeling in 1930, but he redeemed himself against the German in 1932. The latter battle was also filled with controversy, as many felt that the Brandenburg native had the fight. So did Schmeling when I mentioned it to him years later. When the decision went to Sharkey, Schmeling's manager Joe Jacobs coined the phrase "We wuz robbed!"

The great Harry Greb was American light heavyweight titleholder in 1922–23 and world middleweight boxing champion from 1923 to 1926. "The Human/Pittsburgh Windmill" fought 299 times in a thirteen-year career against the best opposition the talent-rich 1910s and '20s could provide him. In December 1919, during the "No-Decision" era, he took on journeyman Mike McTigue in the "Triple Cities." It was one of those bouts that any serious fight fan couldn't miss. The Endicott fisticuffs went in favor of Greb, according to newspaper accounts.

Many area fight fans remember Mike Rossman battling against Binghamton-born Mike Nixon twice in 1975. Californian Nixon first returned home to defeat Tony Berrios at the Broome County Arena in 1973. His second Binghamton battle would be against the undefeated New Jersey

One of America's first sports heroes, Jack Dempsey performs his ring magic against illusionist Harry Houdini. *LC-DIG-ggbain-50392.*

light heavyweight Rossman. Nixon won the split decision against Rossman but lost (KO7) in the rematch a few months later. Rossman eventually got a shot at the light heavyweight championship of the world against Argentine Victor Galindez. In fact, the belt was contested in a bout on the undercard of an Ali-Spinks rematch in September 1978. This event attracted the largest crowd up to that time at an indoor bout. Rossman, considered an underdog by most, fought hard and opened up cuts over Galindez's eyes. Near the end of the thirteenth round, the referee stopped the fight, and Rossman became world champion. As for Nixon, he would end his career with a 1977 fourth-round Garden loss to rising star Vito Antuofermo.

Many who think of middleweights from Binghamton think of Joe Taylor. He fought from 1947 to 1954 and gained quite an area following. Taylor's ring momentum was enhanced in 1948 by two wins over Buffalo's Eli Hall, a draw to Buffalo's Henry Brimm and a victory over Syracuse boxer Nick Barone (1949-W10). Taylor later tackled the likes of J.T. Ross, Lee Sala and Reuben Jones and even landed on some great cards, including one at Yankee Stadium against Artie Towne.

Also battling in and around the "Triple Cities," a mere one hundred miles from "Title Town," were fighters Rocky Kansas, Tommy Ryan, Jim Ryan, Eddie "Babe" Risko, Mickey "Toy Bulldog" Walker and Vito Antuofermo.

BUFFALO

What could be written about the city of Buffalo, less than two hundred miles from Canastota, and its contribution to the "sweet science" could fill volumes.

Abe Attell, Paul Berlenbach, James J. Braddock, Jack Britton, Panama Al Brown, Tony Canzoneri, Kid Chocolate, Jack Delaney, Jack Dillon, Johnny Dundee, Jackie Fields, Tiger Flowers, Joe Gans, Frankie Genaro, Harry Greb, William "Gorilla" Jones, Rocky Kansas, Louis "Kid" Kaplan, Johnny Kilbane, Fidel LaBarba, George "Kid" Lavigne, Benny Leonard, Battling Levinsky, John Henry Lewis, Ted "Kid" Lewis, Tommy Loughran, Charles "Kid" McCoy, Freddie Miller, Battling Nelson, Maxie Rosenbloom, Tommy Ryan, Jimmy Slattery, Mickey Walker, Freddie Welsh, Jess Willard, Kid Williams and Ad Wolgast are a selection of inductees (old-timers) who have fought there. Modern inductees include Henry Armstrong, Ezzard Charles, Joey Giardello, Joe Louis, Lloyd Marshall, Joey Maxim, Carl "Bobo" Olson, Floyd Patterson, Willie Pep, Sugar Ray Robinson, Sandy Saddler,

Jess Willard, a 2003 IBHOF inductee, fought both Jack Johnson and Jack Dempsey. *LC-USZ62-28943.*

"Mysterious" Billy Smith, Jose Torres, Holman Williams, Ike Williams and Fritzie Zivic.

"The Nickel City" had its fair share of heavyweights during the twentieth century, beginning with "the Cinderella Man," James J. Braddock, who knocked out Eddie Benson in the first round of a 1929 Buffalo bout. It was Braddock's last fight before his loss to Tommy Loughran for the light-heavy title in New York City. Later, in 1935, underdog Braddock would win the heavyweight championship of the world in one of the most stunning upsets in boxing history over Max Baer. "The Brown Bomber" also had good luck in Buffalo. Joe Louis kayoed Steve Ketchel in two rounds (1937) and Johnny Davis in one (1944)—a couple of his over-fifty career wins by knockout. Known as "the Cincinnati Cobra," Ezzard Charles is best remembered for his wins as a heavyweight, but most experts feel that he was in his prime as a light heavyweight. He won a decision in Buffalo over Teddy Randolph in 1947 before returning to town in 1950 to face Freddy Beshore. In the National Boxing Association (NBA) title fight, Charles knocked out Beshore in the fourteenth round; this was the fight prior to the New York title shot against Joe Louis. Charles would defeat Louis in a decision to claim both titles. His first title defense would be against a Central New Yorker, Nick Barone, on December 5, 1950, in Cincinnati. Charles was in his prime, and Barone went eleven rounds before succumbing to a knockout.

During the 1920s and 1930s, if the light heavyweight division belonged anywhere, it belonged in Buffalo to a kid coming out of the old First Ward, Jimmy Slattery. Buffalo's golden boy, with his dark hair and Irish charm, captured many hearts in the Empire State. Slattery, son of a Buffalo firefighter, turned pro in 1921 and came up short in his challenge for the world light heavyweight title against Paul Berlenbach in 1925; his KO loss three fights prior to Dave Shade, with his great jab, was named *Ring* magazine "Upset of the Year." Slattery won the vacant NBA light heavyweight title in August 1927, with a decision over Maxie Rosenbloom but lost an attempt at the world title months later to Tommy Loughran.

Three years later, Slattery won the NYSAC world light heavyweight title by beating another Buffalo native, Lou Scozza. He then lost it, and the undisputed world light heavyweight title, to Maxie Rosenbloom the same year; the fifteen thousand fans in attendance loathed the fifteen-round verdict in Buffalo. The United Press score sheet gave Rosenbloom twice as many rounds as "Slatts," with three even. Local Referee Patsy Haley, himself a victim of a Rosenbloom wild swing, opted for Slattery but was overruled by two judges.

"Slapsie Maxie" (Rosenbloom) seemed to like any town, as long as a paycheck was part of the visit. He fought over a dozen times in Buffalo, including bouts with Jimmy Slattery, Art Weigand, Osk Til, Greek Johnson, Harry Fuller, Lou Scozza and Frankie Schoell.

Speaking of the latter pair, Lou Scozza (Scozzaro) and Frankie Schoell—both with over one hundred career battles—fought many outstanding contenders. Scozza (1925–34) holds victories over Jim Braddock and Rosenbloom; Schoell (1918–30) holds them over Rosenbloom and Jack Britton.

Disregarding his corner's advice, Schoell decided to slug it out with the heavier (by thirteen and a half pounds) Jimmy Slattery at the Broadway Auditorium in 1925. His temerity yielded a predictable result: "Slatts" kayoed Schoell in the third round.

As an amateur, Henry Brimm was the 1940 National AAU welterweight champion. The Buffalo native would then go on to win a majority of his nearly fifty professional ring contests. The highlight of his career came in

1949, when he managed a draw against hall of famer Sugar Ray Robinson (1949-D10); he had lost to Robinson the prior year (1948- L10). Before the fight, Brimm had held victories over Leroy Coleman, Artie Towne and Holman Williams. The Buffalo fighter, bolstered by the Robinson draw, decided to tackle both Rocky Graziano and Bobo Olson in 1950. His overconfidence found him horizontal in the fourth round against "the Rock" and at the end of a losing decision to Olson. As for "Sugar Ray," he also fought Jimmy Mandell at the Memorial Auditorium, prior to Brimm, and kayoed him in the fifth round (1945).

Carmine Orlando Tilelli was the middleweight champion of the world from 1963 to 1965 and was better known by his professional pseudonym of Joey Giardello. Prior to his reign, Giardello fought back-to-back bouts against Buffalo's Joey Giambra in 1952. The first fight, in Brooklyn, was a decision victory for Giardello; the rematch, held in Buffalo, was a win for Giambra. They would fight each other three times, the last a 1958 decision in favor of Giambra. Battling from 1949 to 1963, Giambra also fought a pair of noteworthy battles against Rocky Castellani (1956, both wins) and Johnny Sullivan (1956, both wins) at the War Memorial Auditorium in Syracuse, New York. He also fought names such as Bernard Docusen (1953-W7), Jimmy Herring (1953-KO4), Jimmy Welch (1955-W10) and Bobo Olson (1955-L10). In his last Upstate New York battle, which took place at the Memorial Auditorium in Buffalo (1960), Giambra dropped Ralph "Tiger" Jones twice on his way to victory.

Fighting out of the many athletic clubs throughout the area, Frank Erne quickly developed a solid reputation. Born in 1875, he immigrated to the United States from Switzerland and began boxing in the early 1890s. He outpointed George "Kid" Lavigne of Saginaw, Michigan, on July 3, 1899, in a twenty-round lightweight title fight at the Hawthorne Club Arena in Cheektowaga (site of today's Forks Hotel at Broadway and Union Road); the two had tussled nearly a year before and fought to a draw. He would then defend his title against (New York's) Jack O'Brien in an 1899 draw and with a victory via fight stoppage over Joe Gans (1900).

Jimmy Goodrich, born James Edward Moran in Scranton, Pennsylvania, began his professional career about 1918. His first real battle outside Buffalo came against Johnny Dundee in Toronto, Canada (1922-L10). Fighting at a champion's pace, Goodrich lost the split decision in a fight most saw as a draw; his impressive performance was a prelude to his destiny. Three years later, he would win the vacant NYSAC world lightweight title (KO2), having dropped Stan Loayza five times in the first round. Goodrich would keep the title until the last month of the year, when he would lose it in Buffalo to his hometown challenger, Rocky Kansas (1925-L15). Following the Kansas fight, Goodrich would battle until 1930 but never at the intensity he once had.

Rocky Kansas, born Rocco Tozzo on April 21, 1895, in Buffalo, New York, turned pro in 1911 and lost just two official decisions in his first seventy-five fights. In 1914, he faced his first bona fide contenders—Johnny Dundee and Johnny Kilbane—in non-title bouts but lost both decisions. During his career, Kansas tackled the cream of both the featherweight and lightweight divisions, including all-time great Benny Leonard (1916-ND10). When Leonard retired, Kansas was given his third title shot—he had two versus Leonard—this time against Jimmy Goodrich, who claimed the title after Benny's retirement. Kansas was able to get inside on Goodrich and won the 1925 unanimous decision at the Broadway Auditorium. Rocco Tozzo was finally a champion.

During a thirty-four-year period from 1899 to 1933, the city of Buffalo—a focal point for champions—reigned over the professional boxing world with names such as Goodrich, Kansas and Slattery. All were legitimate ring heroes, but none matched the feats, according to some historians, of the outstanding Tommy Paul (Gaetano Alfonso Papa).

After earning the 1927 national AAU bantamweight championship, he turned professional under the watchful eye of Jack Singer and trainer Patsy Newman. From his initial victory in his first fight in 1927, Paul appeared unstoppable. In 1932, he defeated Johnny Pena in Detroit's Olympia Stadium and brought the world featherweight crown home (W15).

Paul's matches with Cincinnati southpaw Freddie Miller quickly became ring legend, and his "hands-down" style was mimicked by many aspiring featherweights. The popular Paul fought many of the best to "lace 'em up," including Fidel LaBarba, Petey Sarron, Frankie Genaro, Panama Al Brown, Kid Chocolate and Bushy Graham.

Buffalo's best, according to historians, included Al Baldesino, Frankie Best, Harris Blake, George (Big Boy) Brackey, Willie (K.O.) Brennan, Henry Brimm, Vic Brown, Sam Butera, Vince Cala, Bud Christiano, Jimmy Clark, Bobby Claus, Dennis (Rocky) Cudney, Ed Cudney, Danny Diliberto, Jackie Donnelly, Jackie Donovan, Jimmy (James) Duffy, Vic Eisen, Frank Erne, Allen Faulkner, Stan Fitzgerald, Art (Tiger) Foster, Rocky Fumerelle, Joey Giambra, Jimmy Gilligan, Joe Gimbrone, Jimmy Goodrich, Johnny Green, Steve Halaiko. Prentiss Hall, Jimmy Harkins, Tommy Hicks, Rocky Kansas, Walter Kolby, Tony Labarbara, Brian Laspada, Horace Leftwich, Joe Matisi,

Leach Cross, one of the many Cross boxing brothers, fought many great fighters, including Lockport's Jimmy Duffy (1913). *LC-DIG-ggbain-10655.*

Bobby Mcquillar, Joe Mesi, Freddie Mueller, Joe Muscato, Phil Muscato, Patsy Newman, George Nichols, Lee Oma, Tommy Paul, Gene Poirerier, Jimmy Ralston, Neal Rivers, Al Rogers, Benny Ross, Bobby Scanlon, Jake Schiffer, Frankie Schoell, Tony Sciolino, Lou Scozza, Jimmy Slattery, Tom Stenhouse, Tommy Tedesco, John (Spider) Thompson, Dick Topinko, Bobby Tracey, Tony Ventura, Jimmy Watkins, Art Weigand, Ted Whitfield and Dick Wipperman.

ROCHESTER

"The Flour City" is a bit over one hundred miles from the boxing shrine in Canastota. Hall of fame members who fought there include (old-timers) Lou Ambers, Jack Delaney, Jack Dillon, Johnny Dundee, Jackie Fields, Frankie Genaro, William "Gorilla" Jones, Rocky Kansas, Louis "Kid" Kaplan, Johnny Kilbane, Battling Levinsky, Ted "Kid" Lewis, Sammy Mandell, Freddie Miller, Maxie Rosenbloom, Tommy Ryan, Jimmy Slattery and

"Fireman" Jim Flynn, a heavyweight contender, fought Tony Ross in Rochester (1915). *LC-DIG-ggbain-10619.*

"Barbados" Joe Walcott, along with modern inductees Carmen Basilio, Ezzard Charles and Joey Maxim.

A few "big guys" made their way through the Flour City, including Primo Carnera, who fought there in 1931—as part of an "Upstate swing"— against Knute Hansen. Like most "Ampling Alp" opponents, Hansen never made it past the first round. Ezzard Charles also made a stop in December 1955, taking a ten-round decision from Toxie Hall.

Bridgeport, Connecticut's Melio Bettina, the former light heavyweight champion (1939), made his last professional fight in Rochester, losing to hometown favorite Johnny Flynn in the sixth round. As for the streaky fighting of John Kowalcyzk, aka Johnny Flynn, he fought from 1939 to 1951, primarily in local arenas and against area fighters, including Buffalo's Lee

Left hook craftsman Charlie White fought throughout Upstate New York. *LC-DIG-ggbain-18068.*

Oma, Endicott's Joe Matisi, Buffalo's Joe Muscato and Buffalo's Billy Nichy.

In 1946, Joey Maxim brought his barrage of left jabs to Rochester to battle Dunkirk's Phil Muscato. It was a given that Muscato, who holds two of the biggest record-drawing crowds at the Buffalo Auditorium, would bring a large contingent east. Maxim would win the fight, but Muscato would win many hearts with his performance.

The talented "Gorilla" Jones took a ten-round contest from Rochester's Abe (Meyer) Lichtenstein in 1930. Lichtenstein first fought out of the Baltimore area before heading north to Rochester, New York, in 1930. He tangled with many Upstate fighters, including Buffalo's Joe Scinta, Buffalo's Freddie Mueller, Syracuse boxer Bucky Lawless, Buffalo's Sam Bruce, Syracuse boxer Jackie Brady and Buffalo's Tony Tozzo.

Teddy Yarosz turned professional in 1929 and won the American middleweight title with a win over Vince Dundee in 1934; the following year, he would lose the belt to Syracuse fighter Eddie "Babe" Risko. He would also battle Jimmy Clark to a ten-round win in Rochester in September 1938 before going on to compete in a fabulous trilogy against Ralph DeJohn (1-2).

He would return to Rochester for his final professional fight on February 2, 1942, losing the contest to Buffalo's Joe Muscato.

Later, Syracuse native Ralph "Rocky" Fratto Jr. would emerge as a contender and fight in three title battles at the Rochester War Memorial Auditorium. Fratto outpointed Rocky Mosley Jr. (1981, NABF junior middleweight title), lost a decision to Tadashi Mihara (1981, vacant WBA junior middleweight title) and won over Chris Linson (1982, NABF junior middleweight title).

Syracuse fighter Bucky Lawless (1924–36), born in Auburn, New York, fought some tough battles at Convention Hall in Rochester, including contests with Joe Dundee (1930-W10) and Young Jack Thompson (1930-W10). Lawless, who engaged in over one hundred ring battles, is perhaps best remembered for a Syracuse battle against Jackie Brady (1930-D) and being managed by Joe Netro.

Sammy Mandell, the handsome "Rockford Sheik," came to Rochester and lost to Auburn-born Steve Halaiko (1930-L8). Mandell, having outpointed Rocky Kansas in a lightweight championship bout held in Chicago on July 3, 1926, had also recently fought Joe Trippe in Buffalo (1930-W10). Halaiko, who compiled over one hundred ring battles (1929-1942), was a gifted light welterweight. In the 1928 Summer Olympics, Halaiko won the silver medal in the lightweight class after losing in the final against Carlo Orlandi. He fought all over Upstate New York and holds victories over many great boxers, including Lou Ambers (1934-W6).

SYRACUSE

The Syracuse (Onondaga County) War Memorial Auditorium is about twenty-five miles from the front door of the International Boxing Hall of Fame. To Canastota's fighters, the facility was a second home.

Hall of fame inductees in the old-timer category who fought in town include Lou Ambers, Abe Attell, Jimmy Barry, Jack Britton, George Dixon, Johnny Dundee, Jackie Fields, Harry Greb, Pete Herman, Rocky Kansas, Johnny Kilbane, Benny Leonard, Battling Levinsky, John Henry Lewis, Ted "Kid" Lewis, Tommy Loughran, Joe Lynch, Sammy Mandell, Charles "Kid" McCoy, Maxie Rosenbloom, Tommy Ryan, Jack Sharkey, "Mysterious" Billy Smith and Freddie Welsh. Modern inductees Carmen Basilio, Ezzard Charles, Kid Gavilan, Billy Graham, Lew Jenkins, Harold Johnson, Sugar Ray Leonard, Jose Napoles, Carlos Ortiz, Willie Pep, Dick Tiger and Ike Williams also battled in Syracuse.

Jack Britton, a 1990 IBHOF inductee, hails from nearby Clinton, New York. *LC-DIG-ggbain-11706.*

"Death Followed a Light Blow from Fitzsimmons' Fist" was just one of the newspaper headlines greeting fight fans on November 19, 1894. The sport's first three-division world champion, Robert Fitzsimmons, delivered a light blow with a right to Con Riordan's jaw during a boxing exhibition. The feckless blow staggered Riordan, who fell to his knees unconscious. Failed efforts to revive him concluded at 3:30 a.m. Fitzsimmons, promptly placed under arrest at 2:15 a.m., was taken to police headquarters.

The bail was set at $10,000, with Fitzsimmons set to answer the charge of manslaughter in the first degree. The first physician on the scene felt that the death had been caused by apoplexy, not the blow. "Yank" Sullivan, who was with Fitzsimmons, offered to post bail for the fighter and agreed that the punch would not have injured a child. The incident caused quite a stir in both the fight community and around town. Although the fighter—perhaps the greatest puncher of all time—was later exonerated of the charges, he would never forget Upstate New York.

At the end of his career, and still suffering from his two 1954 title bout losses to Rocky Marciano, Ezzard Charles took a fight with the six-foot,

Sam McVey, a 1999 IBHOF inductee, was one of the best heavyweights of his era. He fought Sam Langford in Syracuse. *LC-DIG-ggbain-17949.*

three-inch Tommy "Hurricane" Jackson in Syracuse. Managed by Whitey Bimstein, Jackson would give Central New York fight fans something to remember. On August 3, 1955, Jackson decisioned Charles in a hard-fought ten-round battle at the War Memorial Auditorium. Charles, furious over the loss, demanded—and received—a rematch at the end of the month. However, the result of the subsequent encounter would be identical, the only obvious difference being the location: Cleveland. Six months later, Jackson was ranked behind Archie Moore as a contender for Rocky Marciano's heavyweight title.

Rory Calhoun defeated Dick Tiger in Syracuse on July 17, 1959. Calhoun, who resided in White Plains, New York, had fought Tiger to a draw a few weeks earlier in Madison Square Garden. The controversial decision at the auditorium in Syracuse caused the fans of both fighters to rebel. Calhoun had built an Upstate fan base after his local fights against Frenchman Germinal Ballarin (W) and Buffalo's Joey Giambra (D) in 1957. The fierce Tiger, coming off a British tour of middle contenders, was getting his first taste of America, and Calhoun was it!

Minnesota middleweight champ Mike O'Dowd fought Jackie Clark (1919-ND10) and Ted "Kid" Lewis (1919-ND) in the "Salt City." But World War I veteran O'Dowd will always be remembered for his trilogy (2-1) with the prolific, but streaky, Charles Fazio, aka Young Fisher. Fazio, a fixture from about 1915 to 1928, fought in over one hundred bouts. The great Harry Greb also fought Fisher twice in Syracuse during this period (1919-ND10, 1923-W12), with Bill Brennan (1919-ND10) sandwiched between both.

Middleweight Eddie "Babe" Risko (Henry L. Pylkowski), who fought from 1929 to 1939, returned to his birthplace in May 1934. His fights included Clinton's Jackie Flowers (1934-W6), Syracuse boxer Bucky Lawless (1934-W6), Werner Wilsch (1934-KO2), Solvay's Freddie Sallus (1934-D8, 1934-KO8), Benny Levine (1935-KO2), Jackie Aldare (1935-W10), Joe Butch Lynch (1936-KO8) and an "eye-closer" from Ralph DeJohn (1938-KO by 7).

Speaking of the DeJohns, how about Joey? People still refer to his August 17, 1949 loss to Lee Sala at MacArthur Stadium. Sala, coming into the bout at 52-1, was knocked down once in the first round, twice in the fifth and once in the sixth, while DeJohn only suffered a broken jaw! In 1951, DeJohn would avenge his loss by dropping Sala in the second round of a fight at the War Memorial Auditorium.

The first recognized welterweight boxing champion of the world Mysterious Billy Smith brought the weight class into Syracuse before the turn of the century. In many ways, this was the perfect prelude because Smith fought Tom Crawley (1895-ND6) in the city and Tommy Ryan (1896-ND5) at the Alhambra. While Smith was relentless, he was also a dirty fighter. He had two unsuccessful attempts at the world welterweight title in 1894 and 1895; both bouts came against Tommy Ryan (L20, D18), and both battles were held outside Upstate New York.

Following the "Basilio-Backus-Welter era," the frequency of fights declined; however, a few are worth noting, including Saoul Mamby's draw with Johnny Harp (1971-D8) at the War Memorial Auditorium and Sugar Ray Leonard's title defense against Denver's Larry Bonds (1981-KO10) at the Carrier Dome.

Lou Jenkins came to town to battle Carmen Basilio (1950-L10), as did Ike Williams (1953-L10). The latter also fought Syracuse fighter Pat Manzi in a well-publicized ring war. Manzi, who entered the ring with over twenty wins, was dropped by Williams in the seventh round (1952-TKO7). It was a hard-fought battle at the War Memorial and, despite the loss, won Manzi even greater respect. The Syracuse boxer, who battled from 1950 to 1958, also fought Chico Vejar, Tony DeMarco, Joe Miceli and Al Andrews.

Willie Lewis fought around the Albany area and even made a stop in Glens Falls to tackle Bill Hurley. *LC-DIG-ggbain-08232*.

The city of Syracuse hosted some outstanding turn-of-the-century featherweight battles, beginning with George Dixon's bout against Tommy White at the Empire Athletic Club (1898-D20). The quick and agile Dixon was one of the all-time greats. He was also the first black fighter to capture a world title, defeating Nunc Wallace for the vacant bantamweight title on June 27, 1890, in London, England. Tommy White would later fight to victory for the American 126-pound title at the Monarch Athletic Club in Syracuse (1898-W20).

UTICA

The city of Utica is situated in the Mohawk Valley and the Leatherstocking region. Some of the hall of fame fighters who battled here include George Foreman, Frankie Genaro, Sammy Mandell, Battling Nelson, Willie Pep, Jose Torres and "Barbados" Joe Walcott. Other notables include Jackie Flowers, Mike McTigue, Eddie "Babe" Risko, Steve Wolanin and Bobby Wilson.

Heavy snows detoured 1908 Great Race drivers, pictured here in Utica, to the Erie Canal towpath—another sport finding solace along the waterway. LC-*DIG-ggbain-00154.*

Philadelphia's prolific Johnny Jadick, a light welterweight, visited the city in 1936 to clash with Angelo Geraci, aka Bushy Graham. The tough Utica fighter, who stood five feet, five inches tall, had to "step up" in weight to take the fight. But in typical Graham style, he dropped Jadick three times during the Utica Stadium victory (W8).

Angelo Geraci was born in Italy about 1905 and named after his paternal grandfather. The eldest of five brothers, he would be the first to nurture his physical abilities inside a ring; his brother Frankie also boxed. Impressed by the pocket change he could earn from boxing, he quickly applied for a boxing license. Turning pro in the early twenties, he never fought outside Upstate New York until 1924, and then it was under the name Mickey Garcia. Naturally, the use of assumed names—he also used Bobby Garcia—can inhibit the completion of earlier records; that is, until a moniker, such as Bushy Graham, finally sticks. In 1924, he fought future flyweight champion Frankie Genaro to a draw in Rochester, New York. His performance was enough to impress many, and a rematch was promptly scheduled. Two months later, this time in Brooklyn, Genaro defeated Graham by decision. The result did little to impede Graham, who rattled off a string of victories over many, including Nat Pincus, Phil Verdi, Larry Goldberg, Eddie O'Dowd and Abe Goldstein. In 1925, Graham fought future bantamweight champion Bud Taylor twice, first to a "no-decision" and then to a win. Positioning himself for a title shot would be his next crusade—political roadwork that could also have its pugilistic pitfalls.

In 1928, Graham fought for and won both the vacant NYSAC and NBA bantamweight titles in a bout held at Ebbet's Field in Brooklyn, New York, against Corporal Izzy Schwartz. Throughout the first ten rounds, Schwartz held his ground against his larger opponent, but he finally succumbed under the punishing pace. Graham would win his next four fights before losing to Fidel LaBarba (1928-L10). Following the LaBarba

In 1911, Battling Nelson, a 1992 IBHOF inductee, fought in both Buffalo and Utica. *LC-DIG-ggbain-04071.*

fight, he would lose fewer than ten fights, only to quality opponents such as Kid Chocolate, Andy Martin, Bat Battalino, LaBarba again, Tommy Paul and Enrico Venturi—all on the way to over one hundred victories.

Luigi Giuseppe D'Ambrosio, aka Lou Ambers, was born on November 8, 1913. A talented lightweight boxer, the "Herkimer Hurricane" fought from 1932 to 1941. If aptitude draws expertise, then Ambers is certainly exemplary. He was managed by Nicanor Rafael (1932–33), Dave Steinberg (1933–34) and, later, Al Weill (1934–41). The latter managed four world champions—Rocky Marciano, Marty Servo, Ambers and Joey Archibald. Ambers was trained by a trio: Al Silvani, who trained over twenty world champions; Charley Goldman, who worked with Al McCoy and Rocky Marciano; and Whitey Bimstein, who worked with Fred Apostoli, Joey Archer and Jim Braddock.

Ambers was an aggressive fighter and a tactician, not taking a loss until May 7, 1934, at the hands of Buffalo's Steve Halaiko in Syracuse. His memorable Utica battles include Cleveland's Frankie Wallace (1933-W6), Syracuse boxer Eddie Dempsey (1934-KO3, Mohawk) and Buffalo's Mickey Paul (1934-KO4).

On May 10, 1935, Ambers faced lightweight champion Tony Canzoneri, the youngest featherweight ever. Although he would lose the decision (L15), the Utica fighter was far from discouraged. Ambers won his next fourteen fights and then vindicated himself by capturing the lightweight championship in a rematch with Canzoneri (1936-W15).

On August 17, 1938, Ambers met Henry Armstrong in a historic title fight in New York City. Armstrong, a perpetual punching machine, was attempting to become the first fighter in history to win and hold three world titles simultaneously—not an easy task! In an epic battle, Ambers was knocked down twice by "Homicide Hank" in the fifth and sixth rounds and appeared defeated. Although he mounted an impressive comeback, Ambers lost the controversial split decision. A rematch was inevitable and came in August 1939, again at the Garden. In a dogfight as disputable as their first bout, Referee Donovan penalized Armstrong five rounds for low blows. But Ambers, who never capitulated, captured the fifteen-round decision in his final great performance.

By 1940, the winds of the "Herkimer Hurricane" had diminished. An attempt at defending his title against the wild, free-swinging Lew Jenkins failed. Ambers, who was knocked out in the third round, had hit the canvas four times during the upset. An obligatory rematch followed on February 28, 1941, again at Madison Square Garden. Jenkins, now with nearly fifty wins under his belt, knocked Ambers down twice in the seventh for a TKO victory.

As impressive as it is extensive, our brief assessment of Upstate New York's boxing heritage ends here in Utica, less than thirty-five miles from "Title Town, USA."

3

Boxing in Upstate New York

The People

In boxing, success is often achieved when preparation welcomes opportunity. While a fighter is being readied, all of the components surrounding a fight need to be carefully prepared. It is an arduous undertaking involving many individuals, such as managers and trainers—pugilistic pundits with specific roles. Once complete, it is then, and only then, that a chance is welcome. But that opportunity, that fight, must present itself, and that involves even more people—promoters, matchmakers, referees, announcers, newsmen, etc.—all with specific roles that, too, must be conducted with pugilistic proficiency. In providing this talent—exceptional individuals in all aspects of the fight game—Upstate New York has shined brightest.

With such a rich boxing heritage, what better way to reflect on the sport itself than to tell its history through the many participants who have called Upstate New York their home—individuals, reflective of an era, who chose a pugilistic path. They were our neighbors, our friends and even our heroes.

EARLY BOXING ROOTS

Choosing a couple of individuals to define our boxing roots is like trying to pick a favorite American Patriot. Do I pick Patrick Henry or Thomas Jefferson? Many names come to mind: Billy Baker (1883–92), Tom Couhig (1899–1904), Frank Erne (1891–1908), Jack Hamilton (trainer), Captain Jim Wescott (manager), Eddie Franklin (manager) and Bobby Smith (manager). But I just can't escape two.

William Muldoon was born on May 25, 1845, in the Genesee Valley district of New York State known as Belfast (Allegheny County). He would become a wrestling champion, a physical fitness expert and the first chairman of the New York State Athletic Commission (NYSAC). Nicknamed "the Solid Man," Muldoon established himself as an advocate of physical fitness and a Greco-Roman wrestling champion. In 1889, inside a Belfast barn, he trained boxer John L. Sullivan for his famous seventy-five-round fight against Jake Kilrain for the world heavyweight bare-knuckle championship. When Sullivan won, Muldoon gained national acclaim for restoring the boxing champion to peak fighting form—a task at the time dismissed by the press as not plausible.

Despite boxing's immense popularity, after the Civil War, it was still illegal in many states, including New York. This meant that matchmakers—those who put the fights together—had to conduct their business discreetly in places such as Harry Hill's Club in New York City. There they planned ring battles for discreet locations such as the backroom of a club, inside a barn or even on a barge in international waters. The goal was to attract a large audience for the best talent attainable. Muldoon's training methodology would evolve through his days as a health farm proprietor in Westchester County and his service on NYSAC. A mainstay in New York sports for over fifty years, his commemorative plaque resides inside the walls of the International Boxing Hall of Fame.

Redwood, New York, rests in the eastern part of the town of Alexandria, where harsh winters are as common as lumber camps. Joseph Youngs—some sources spell it Younges—was born there in 1870 to a French father and English mother. The family moved to Syracuse, New York, Joseph recalls, when he was still a youth. In the "Salt City," a man named Meyers used to keep a saloon on Railroad Street, and every Saturday night there would be a couple of short bouts in the barroom. He would sneak in to observe the action (age forbade him to be a known observer). It was there that the taste of the "sweet science" left its mark.

By fifteen, he was acting as a water boy for one of the construction gangs on the Toledo & Ann Arbor Railway in Michigan. It was among the railway laborers that he got his first chance at fighting. The skintight leather gloves seemed to fit perfectly, and the sport came naturally to the youth. He learned the first movements of sidestepping, feinting and parrying, which, once refined, would gain him boxing acclaim. Since the camps, each with its own champion, would stage bouts, it was the perfect proving ground. There were no rounds, only a start signal; no padded canvas floors, only what was

Jim Jeffries, who retired undefeated, was coaxed back into the ring and suffered his only loss to Jack Johnson. *LC-DIG-ggbain-08034.*

Syracuse boxer Tommy Ryan, born in Redwood, New York, fought often in Upstate New York. *LC-DIG-ggbain-08063.*

underfoot; and a fight ended when an opponent was knocked out or simply gave up.

Youngs began boxing professionally in 1887. In a career that would last for two decades, the scrappy fighter and strong puncher quickly rose to the heights of the welterweight ranks. On July 26, 1894, in Minneapolis, he took the welterweight championship by defeating Mysterious Billy Smith in twenty rounds. He later entered the middleweight division and laid claim to the crown vacated by the great Robert Fitzsimmons. From 1895 to 1900, he fought numerous times in Upstate New York, and his opponents included Syracuse boxer Joe Dunfee (Empire Athletic Club, Buffalo) and Jim Ryan (Maple Avenue Athletic Club, Elmira). Jack Dempsey, Bill Payne and Jack Bonner were also ring victims. Later, he traveled the vaudeville circuit and performed boxing exhibitions with Robert Fitzsimmons. He also spent time managing fighters, trained James J. Jeffries and even ran a gym in Syracuse, New York. When the bell tolled for him in Van Nuys, California, on August 3, 1948, it rang for a name never to be forgotten—that of future hall of fame member Tommy Ryan.

1910s

America came of age during this time period. Reform was on the mind of many, and social issues were common: immigration, labor, poverty, suffrage and work safety. The War to End All Wars raged, as did some terrific fighters, including Steve Morrisey (1897–1911), Charley Hitte (1899–1912), Tom McCarthy (1890–1912), Rochester's Mike Donovan (1897–1912), Paddy Lavin (1904–14), Battling Gates (1910–16), Kid Henry (1908–16), Al Fisher (1912–18), Bill Hurley (1908–19), Harry Baker (1906–19) and Kid Curley (1904–19).

Patsy Haley was born in July 1877, in Newmarket Juncture, New Hampshire. His father, who happened to own the Bijou concert hall in Buffalo, New York, introduced him to the sport of boxing. For Haley, amateur success led to turning professional by the fall of 1894. He battled and won a majority of over seventy-five bouts. His last Upstate ring battle was against the popular hometown fighter Joe Goldberg at the Olympic Athletic Club in Rochester, New York. After ending his ring career in 1914, and having fought the likes of hall of fame members George Dixon, Abe Attell and Terry McGovern, Haley was appointed a referee by the NYSAC. It was inside the ropes once again that he would hear another calling, that of an arbiter. During the early days of the Walker Law, he was quick to establish an estimable reputation—not an easy task in this era. Haley refereed numerous championship bouts, including Kid Chocolate v. Lew Feldman (1932-KO12), Frankie Genaro v. Midget Wolgast (1930-D15) and even the controversial Maxie Rosenbloom v. Jimmy Slattery (1930-W15). With his combed-back white hair, bow tie and pressed slacks, he set the standard for many an acclaimed adjudicator.

Born in Lockport on June 12, 1889, Jimmy Duffy was a lanky character who stood nearly six feet tall. With orthodox stance, a solid left and good reach, his opponents often cringed when viewing his chiseled frame. Turning pro in 1908, he grappled in the usual haunts, including small halls and athletic clubs, honing his skills and even fighting good area talent such as Herman Smith, Henry "Fighting" Zunner and Joe Tozzo, aka Joe "Kid" Kansas. The latter was the oldest of the three battling Tozzo brothers; the other two were Rocco "Rocky" Kansas and the youngest, Tony. By 1912, Duffy was stepping up to names like Freddie Welsh, Knockout Brown, Leach Cross and even Packey McFarland. He took back-to-back battles over Jack Britton at the Broadway Auditorium in Buffalo and honed his skills against Charley White and Freddie Welsh.

From 1915 to 1920, he fought Johnny Dundee; Ted "Kid" Lewis three times, including for the world welterweight title; Jack Britton three times; and Benny Leonard, promoted as world lightweight title. His final Upstate

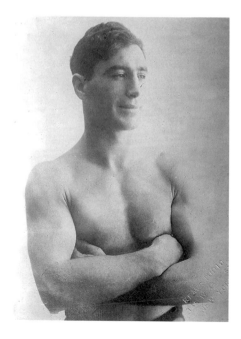

Masterful boxer Jack Britton fought nemesis Ted "Kid" Lewis in Buffalo (1916) as part of a twenty-fight rivalry. *LC-DIG-ggbain-13382.*

New York ring battle, also his last professional fight, came on January 21, 1921, against another Tozzo—Rocco—who turned Duffy's lights out in the first round. Duffy served as a Niagara County sheriff's deputy from 1922 to 1949, and as time has passed, his ring legacy has appreciated.

1920s

The Roaring Twenties saw a return to "political normalcy" in the wake of World War I. The Walker Law, sponsored by Senator James J. Walker and adopted in 1920, once again legalized professional boxing in New York State. Jazz music blossomed, the flapper redefined modern womanhood and art deco peaked—all before the Wall Street Crash of 1929 served to punctuate the end of the era and usher in the beginning of the Great Depression. The popularity of both Jack Dempsey and Gene Tunney helped spawn the birth of the *Ring* magazine on February 15, 1922. It would quickly become boxing's premier communication conduit.

This was a prolific fighting period with so many great names: Jake Schiffer (1911–21), Al Rogers (1908–21), (Henry) Fighting Zunner (1910–22), Willie Brennan (1905–22), George "Young" Erne (1910–23), Battling Kopin (1912–23), Nick Michaels (Vercillo) (1914–25), Battling Hurley (1915–25), Chief Halftown (1916–26), Bud Christiano (1917–27), Young Fisher (Charles Fazio, 1915–28), Harry Cook (1917–28), Canastota Bob (Joe Kanafolo, 1921–29), Mike Conroy (1920–29) and Allie Smith (manager). But two diverse favorites come to mind.

Born on September 27, 1901, in Philadelphia, Roy Simmons attended Hydes Park High School in Chicago. There, he fell in love with sports—all sports. His fascination with athletics took him even further at Syracuse University. He began his coaching career in 1925, soon after graduation, and made a name for himself in boxing, football and lacrosse. Although his sporting prowess is often associated with a field, he was equally capable in a ring. As coach of the Syracuse University varsity boxing team from 1925 until 1956, when the school dropped the sport, his team won an impressive fourteen Eastern Championships.

Alexander J. Brown of Rochester, New York, proved that even during a turbulent era one could still be a gentleman in the sport of boxing. Born on November 8, 1894, Brown didn't begin fighting professionally until 1920. Like most, he tackled the local undercard talent first—area fighters like Jimmy Turner, Joe Hurley and Mixer Mitchell, along with Jamestown's Phil

James J. Walker sponsored the law that legalized boxing in New York State. *LC-DIG-ggbain-37837*.

Logan—before "moving up" to names like Buffalo's Jimmy Goodrich and Rocky Kansas. In 1924, Brown fought Canastota Bob (Joseph Kanafolo) at the arena in Syracuse to a six-round draw. The winner was to lay a claim on the Central New York lightweight title. From that point forward, his skill seemed to wane a bit, forcing him to hang up the gloves in February 1928. His last Upstate New York battle was against Buffalo boxer Jack Oakes inside the Broadway Auditorium in Buffalo on May 6, 1927. "Chubby" Brown was often recalled as "the Chesterfield of the Ring" for his gentlemanly manners. He is still considered one of Rochester's best fighters of all time.

1930s

In a decade with its first few years marked by the Great Depression, the economy had a traumatic effect on Upstate New York and the world. The period also saw a proliferation of new technologies, including intercontinental aviation and radio. In the fight of the decade, Jack Dempsey floored Luis Firpo seven times in the first round. But it was the Argentine giant's second knockdown of the defending champion that will live forever. A powerful right sent Dempsey through the ropes, and aided by a group of ringside observers, the champ barely reentered the ring by the count of ten. But Firpo never followed up, and the champ was champ for a reason. Dempsey scored a kayo one round later.

Upstate New York was rich in talent, including Joe Banovic (1926–40), Charlie Pinto (Panepinto, 1925–30), Frisco Grande (1923–32), Johnny McCoy (1916–32), Joe Trippe (1926–33), Jackie Brady (1920–33), Steve Wolanin (1925–34), Osk Till (1923–34), Johnny Sacco (1924–34), Sam Bruce (1924–35), Frankie Garcia (Geraci, 1924–36), Tony Tozzo (1927–37), Bucky Lawless (1925–37), Tony Paul (Vito Papa, 1932–39), Eddie "Babe" Risko (1929–39) and George Nichols (1923–39), not to mention others involved in the sport.

In Buffalo, the names of Slattery (1921–34) and Goodrich were as common as a cold winter. So were many of the names that surrounded the sport during this time—individuals like Paul "Red" Carr, the amateur lightweight boxer and manager of both. Before turning to managing, Carr also battled as a pro featherweight for a brief time around town.

An amateur fighter, manager, promoter, matchmaker and owner of Singer's Gym, Jack Singer's name was also common in Buffalo fight circles. The gym operated at 1385 Sycamore Street and remained there until 1929. Singer then moved it to 577 Main Street and then on to 338 Washington Street (early 1930s). Following World War I, Singer fought as an amateur boxer before becoming a manager. Under his watchful eye, he altered the careers of Tommy Paul, George Nichols, Terry Meyers, Frankie Linhart, Tony Stabeneau and Mickey Paul (Tommy Paul's brother).

Having briefly been involved with the Silver Leaf Athletic Club, he enjoyed the promotional side of the sport as well and returned to it in 1943. Singer organized the Hudson Boxing Club in partnership with Tom Lippes. During the next eight years, the club played a major role in the revival of boxing in Western New York. The club events expanded from the Eagles Auditorium and the Civic Stadium into the Old Vienna Theatre and then on to the Memorial Auditorium, where they would stay well into the 1950s. Singer was also essential in bringing some of boxing's top stars to Buffalo.

Other boxing names also come to mind when one thinks of Jack Singer, including Hugh Shannon, boxing promoter, manager and matchmaker; fight manager Tommy Timlin; and the beloved Bert Finch. The latter spent over a half century watching over the likes of Lou Scozza, Jimmy Duffy, Frankie Schoell, Bobby Tracey, Elmer Doane, Tommy Moore, Chip Davis,

Teddy Meyers, Joey Joynt, Johnny Sacco, Mike Martyk, Joe Matisi and others. At one time, Finch's stable of fighters was one of the largest in the state of New York. He was so cherished for his contribution to the sport that over four hundred people attended a dinner held in his honor on June 16, 1953, at the Hotel Buffalo.

Another fighter of the era was known as the "Fighting Altar Boy," a talented puncher out of Niagara Falls. Born there on July 29, 1916, Tommy Tedesco was the youngest of ten children. He served as an altar boy at St. Joseph's Catholic Church on Pine Avenue and attended the school there. A teenager at the height of the Depression, he also looked to boxing for answers.

In 1936, he fought Andy Scrivani of Chicago before a sellout crowd of sixteen thousand at Chicago Stadium for the lightweight spot on the 1936 U.S. Olympic boxing team. Scrivani was awarded a split decision, but his opponent earned a position as a team alternate. That permitted him to sail with the team from New York City to Berlin. He even struck up a friendship with track star Jesse Owens. Scrivani lost his match in the Olympics to a German opponent who would later be kayoed by the "Fighting Altar Boy." Tedesco turned pro in 1937 but never became the champion he wanted to be. He touched many lives in Buffalo, and people were proud to have Tommy Tedesco as a friend.

If the "sweet science" has a soul, it comes in the form of individuals such as Monsignor Franklin Kelliher. A star athlete who matriculated at Holy Cross in Worcester, Massachusetts, he found solace in the art of self-defense. For two years, he was the school's heavyweight boxing champion. He worked tirelessly, honing his skills into a top amateur contender—priesthood and pugilism, who would have thought?

In June 1930, he was ordained a priest and assigned to the Buffalo Diocese. An association with Robert Bibber McCoy, one of the top professional wrestlers in North America, led to a part-time career as a professional wrestler. From 1928 to 1932, his "altar" ego surfaced as the "Masked Marvel" and, later, the "Red Devil." Working exclusively in Montreal, Toronto, Cleveland and occasionally in Buffalo, his career, and the charitable earnings that came with it, came to a dramatic close when his identity was revealed by an opponent. In 1936, Father Kelliher, an assistant pastor at St. John the Baptist Church, was asked by Monsignor Edmond Britt to take over the directorship of the poorly disciplined Working Boys Home. He accepted this position and held it for the next thirty-nine years.

Kelliher, like many, felt that discipline could be acquired through participation in sports, especially boxing. Beginning in 1938, the fifty-boy home would enter a team of boxers in the local Golden Gloves tournament. Boxing shows were also conducted regularly and promoted to generate additional funds. When the *Buffalo Courier Express* dropped its sponsorship of the Golden Gloves in 1960, Kelliher acquired sponsorship of Buffalo's premier amateur boxing event; poor health would eventually preclude him from further participation. Monsignor Franklin Kelliher was an inspiration to many, and when he passed away on February 22, 1985, the sport lost a soul mate.

Ralph DeJohn was born in Syracuse, New York, in 1917 and fought professionally from 1936 to 1947. He was the oldest of the fighting DeJohn boys from Central New York. Instead of starting his career slowly and working up in talent, DeJohn dove right into the Buffalo fight picture by facing an experienced Tony Tozzo and an undefeated Paulie Mahoney. If his intent was to have an immediate impact on local sports, he was certainly successful. His first loss didn't come until April 1937, and it was against his nemesis Jimmy Clark. DeJohn's four fights with Jamestown's Clark in 1937, all at the Broadway Auditorium in Buffalo, were some of the finest of the period.

Stanley Ketchel is considered by some to be the greatest middleweight ever. *LC-DIG-ggbain-01676.*

DeJohn's three fights against New York's Walter Woods in Syracuse (1938–39) were also fierce battles, as were his encounters with Pennsylvania's Teddy Yarosz. DeJohn's final professional fight came against Chubby Wright at MacArthur Stadium in Syracuse on August 28, 1947. He took the eight-round win to complete his outstanding seventy-fight career; it stands at 52-15-3.

1940S

World War II took place in the first half of the decade and had a profound effect on most countries and people in Europe, Asia and elsewhere. Joe Louis was the fighter of the decade, although the war left little time for fistic heroics. In an effort to stem the Great Depression, the government pumped money into public works, such as Buffalo's replacement for the aging Broadway Auditorium. A haven for boxing, and the city's only convention spot, the new auditorium was to be located between Lower Terrace and Lake Streets—a spot in the oldest part of Buffalo that was once the Erie Canal. The cornerstone was laid on November 30, 1939.

A flood of names—the list is endles, just look at Buffalo alone—comes to mind when you think about this period: Eddie Dempsey (1929–40), Joe Gerace (1931–43), Bill Nichy (1932–45), Billy Pinti (1939–47) and Carmine Casale (1929–47). But so do places.

For decades, beginning in the 1940s and ending in the '70s, the Catskill Mountain region of New York State, commonly referred to as "the Borscht Belt," was a weekend and holiday destination for scores of New Yorkers. Resorts adorned the glorious landscape, including the Concord, Kutsher's and Grossinger's. In fact, it was the fighter and war hero Barney Ross who really put the latter site on the map as a boxing training facility. Others soon followed, including Rocky Marciano, Emile Griffith, Jerry Quarry, Ken Norton and Gerry Cooney. It became an added attraction and an accepted tradition to have great boxers training in the Catskills. No reference to Upstate New York boxing would be complete without reference to Jennie Grossinger's smile and the inclusion of this famed facility.

It was said that if you lived in Syracuse during the '40s, you either knew a DeJohn or fought with one, or you fought with someone who did. Joey DiGianni was born on November 21, 1926. As a member of the DeJohn clan, which included brothers Ralph (whom you already met), Carmen, Mike, Tommy, Lou and John, boxing was in his blood. When school no longer sat well with him—or perhaps through a bit of coaxing from his brothers—he decided to pursue boxing full time and turned professional in 1944. Joey was also a World War II United States Navy boxer.

As a middleweight, he was energetic, powerful and packed a solid left hook. The "Golden Boy" compiled an impressive record of 74-14-2, which included a string of over twenty-five victories and an astounding fifty-two knockouts. As one fan put it, "He was a knockout artist—when he wasn't painting the canvas with his opponent, he was doing it himself."

DeJohn's first major opponent came in the form of Pete Mead in December 1947. The Grand Rapids middleweight brought his impressive 29-7 record into the Memorial Auditorium in Buffalo. Although he was floored in the second round, Mead disposed of his opponent in the sixth. The defeat only proved to spark DeJohn, who went on another impressive streak of eighteen straight victories.

On February 25, 1949, DeJohn would confront Mead again, this time at Madison Square Garden in New York City. DeJohn came out strong and by the end of the fifth had dropped Mead twice. But DeJohn was tiring, and his aggressive strategy found him exhausted by the seventh. Once Mead dropped him for the third time that round, the fight was over. Fifty years later, most historians ranked the battle among their "Top Ten Great Madison Square Garden Fights."

As everyone knew by now, DeJohns don't lose; they are simply reactivated. Joey battled Jake LaMotta (1949-L8) and then went on to vindicate himself, finally, against Pete Mead (1949-KO7) in their third battle, this time held at Red Wing Stadium in Rochester, New York. This was "classic DeJohn"—lose to an opponent and then come back solid with a victory. Other such examples followed: Lee Sala, lost by knockout (1949) and then won by knockout (1951); Joe Taylor, lost in a split decision (1950) and then won in a third-round knockout (1951); and Henry Lee, lost in a decision (1951) and then won by knockout (1952). He kept Syracuse in the fight game, brought considerable talent to the area and polished a great family legacy that still shines to this day.

Bobby Claus, born on September 25, 1920, was a streaky welterweight from Buffalo, New York. He fought from 1941 to 1949 at all of the local venues. He managed his way into matches against much better fighters, including welter Jimmy Doyle of Jamaica, New York's Bobby Lakin and even the great Tony Zale, not once but twice (1946 and 1948). The results were the same—all losses, most by knockout. But Claus was bound for Buffalo immortality.

Boxing in Upstate New York: The People

As the turbulent decade ended, local fight fans couldn't stop talking about the Rocky Graziano v. Bobby Claus bout held on June 21 at Wilmington Park, Wilmington, Delaware—the only place that would license "the Rock." Rocky headed into the fight at 47-8-5, primed and looking for a reason, any reason, to avenge the humiliation of his last bout, a middleweight title fight against Tony Zale, who sent Graziano to the stars in the third round. In one of those fights, not expected to be much of a battle at all, fans witnessed Buffalo's own Bobby Claus drop the controversial Graziano to the count of two in the very first round. Nobody could believe it. Claus, at 13-18-1, far from a match for the stylish Graziano, stunned his opponent and perhaps himself. But a Graziano fight is never over until the referee declares it so, and everyone witnessing the fight knew it. A vigilant Claus, in what would be his final professional fight, took five nine counts before being knocked out in the second round. Coincidentally, when both fighters had last faced common opponent Tony Zale—both having kissed the canvas, by the way—it was Claus who had lasted longer by a round.

Born and raised in Buffalo's old First Ward, the same district that produced Leo Maher, Jimmy Slattery and Jackie Donovan, was a young kid with promise. In 1941, at age sixteen, he won the New York Golden Gloves Tournament of Champions in the bantamweight division. A protégé of the great Jimmy Slattery and tutored by Lou Wertheimer, the youngster showed enormous promise before turning pro in January 1943. But ring promise was soon overshadowed by world conflict. In a reminder to us all of cost of freedom, Lester H. McGowan was killed in action at Iwo Jima during World War II.

From 1947 to 1954, if you were talking boxing in Binghamton, you probably included the name Joe Taylor. Fighting out of the Kalurah Temple, he struggled his first year as a pro before battling his way up the welterweight ranks. On January 12, 1949, he stepped up, both in weight and caliber of opponent, when he took on tough Syracuse boxer Nick Barone at the Kalurah Temple in Binghamton. Taking advantage of Barone's bruised right hand, Taylor took the ten-round decision. Barone, never an easy fight for any opponent, was tough even with only one good glove. Taylor then took his following fight against New York's Tony Masciarelli before losing to a healthy—"I told ya so!"—Barone in a controversial Syracuse rematch.

Despite his first loss to Barone, Taylor was now on his game, posting wins over solid competitors. Even his losses were impressive: Lee Sala (1949-L10), Artie Towne (1949-KO8) and Jake LaMotta (1950-L10). But Taylor was a streaky fighter who could get a bit overconfident at the wrong time. He took a third fight with Nick Barone in August 1950. Now, as any Syracuse fight fan will tell you, it's fair to take a second fight with Barone; it's suicide to take a third, especially in Syracuse. Barone took a ten-round unanimous decision, and Taylor took a terrible pounding. For years, many a ring tale was spun at Gentlemen Joe's in Binghamton about the saloon's owner and his brother.

1950s

With manufacturing and home construction on the rise, the United States economy was on the upswing, as was the American family. The Korean War and the beginning of the Cold War created a politically conservative climate, but the social climate would be far different with the advent of rock 'n' roll. Building continued, including the Onondaga War Memorial, a 6,230-seat multipurpose arena in downtown Syracuse. It would feature the first poured-in-place concrete roof in the United States and would host some fighters who may have come from the same mold. The facility would never entertain the fighter of the decade, Sugar Ray Robinson, because it didn't need to. It had its own by the name of Carmen Basilio.

Upstate New York's "Golden Age" had many great names attached, including Joey Kushner (1931–50), Joe Tambe (1933–50), Johnny Flynn (1939–51), Nick Barone (1946–51), Barney Taylor (1947–51), Rolly Johns (1947–51), Ross Virgo (1948–52), Frankie Basil (1948–53), Jimmy DeMura (1949–59), Bobby Scanlon (1954–66) and too many others to mention. The same is true outside the ring: Joseph Cardenia (promotion), Charley

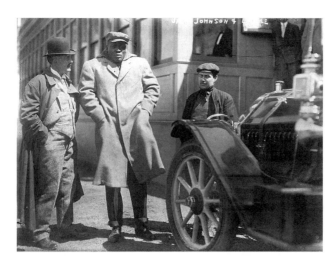

Jack Johnson, the first African American heavyweight champion, was inducted into the IBHOF as part of the 1990 inaugural class. *LC-DIG-ggbain-0898.*

Murray (promoter), Dick Tobin (Syracuse War Memorial Auditorium ring announcer), Thomas A. Coulter (Olympic coach), Ray Rinaldi (trainer, coach), Terry Dundon (coach), Phil Serling (manager), Don Hamilton (boxer, historian), Charlie Basile (referee), Freddie Stanton (referee) and Irving "Irv" Robbins (gym owner, coach).

On March 6, 1952, Norman Rothschild promoted his first fight at the War Memorial Auditorium in Syracuse, New York. The bout, an outstanding card for any rookie backer, was between local favorite Joey DeJohn and the fierce French middleweight Robert Villemain. Rothschild, who organized the Arena Boxing Club, Inc., in 1951, had grown close to both the sport and its participants. But promoting is always a challenge, both working in a new facility and in a sport such as boxing, particularly during the 1950s. Rothschild quickly identified the provocations and overcame the obstacles to become a recognized impresario, backing ten championship fights starting in 1959, as well as an early advocate of the use of television as a vehicle for the fight game. Boxing historians often wonder what the Central New York fight scene would have been like, or whether it would have even existed, had it not been for the talents of this man.

1960s

Social and political upheaval was not limited to any country during the 1960s; everyone shared in the confusion. The Beatles arrived in America, as did an abundance of liberal attitudes and drug experimentation. As the counterculture of the era was trying to find itself, a new set of heroes emerged. A young Cassius Marcellus Clay Jr. was as one of those new icons. Like his ring predecessors, John L. Sullivan, Jack Dempsey, Joe Louis and Sugar Ray Robinson, his impact would be felt for decades, both in and outside of the ring.

Across the Empire State, contributors emerged, including Stan Fitzgerald (1955–61), Willie Bell (1957–61), Johnny Pratt (1949–62), Jackie Donnelly (1958–63), Al Simmons (1958–67), Dick Wipperman (1961–68), Tommy Hicks (1967–74), Eddie Beauford (1969 national Golden Gloves light welterweight champion), Joyce Carol Oates (author), Patrick (Pat) Francis Anthony Nolan Putnam (writer, historian), Frank Wakefield (writer) and Paul Wielopolski (coach).

A child was born in Syracuse on Christmas Day 1924, a mere sixty-six miles from the city of Binghamton, New York, the place he would call home.

His family lived on the west side of the city at 67 Bennett Avenue and later in an apartment on Chapin Street. While attending Hamilton Elementary Grade School, West Junior High School and Binghamton Central High School, he expressed interest in a variety of subjects, including writing and sports, especially boxing. As editor of his school newspaper, he would write about nearly everything, always exhibiting a fascination for the dramatic element of a situation. Like many, he joined the armed forces at the advent of World War II. During basic training, he boxed to improve his defensive skills and perhaps to pick up some extra pocket money. Following the war, his career as a playwright hit a pinnacle during the golden age of television. He won the Emmy award for *Requiem for a Heavyweight*, the first original ninety-minute drama ever written expressly for television. It told the story of a once-promising but now washed-up boxer who faces the end of his career after he is savagely defeated. As Binghamton's favorite son, Rod Serling never forgot Upstate New York and the sport he so passionately loved.

The "Ali era" sparked many heavyweight hopefuls in gyms all over the world. In Upstate New York, there were a few; Buffalo's Dick Wipperman

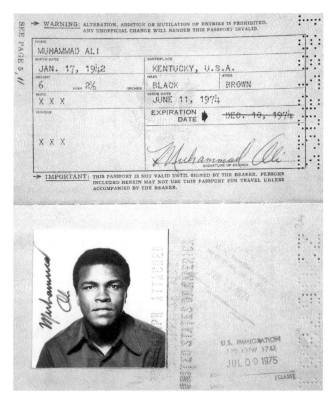

The most recognized international sports figure ever, Muhammad Ali. *Courtesy of Heritage Auctions.*

comes to mind, but so does Syracuse boxer Mike DeJohn, who clearly draws the most similarities to Ali. They shared eight common opponents—Ali defeated them all, while DeJohn defeated only half. Ali TKO'd Alex Miteff in 1961, nine fights into his pro career while on the rise. DeJohn knocked Miteff out in the first round of a 1957 battle, peaking thirty-eight fights into his pro career. So why not DeJohn versus Ali? Perhaps the timing was off. DeJohn had more experience than the opponents Ali was facing at the time, or maybe it was simply boxing politics. But clearly, DeJohn was a contender from the time he dropped Miteff, ranked in the top ten, and during Ali's early rise to fame. Had DeJohn's battle with George Chuvalo ended differently (1963-L10) in Louisville, of all places, maybe things would have been different. The loss sent DeJohn into retirement. A victory over the tough Canadian, whom Ali fought twice, might have meant a match for DeJohn. It's just hard to say for sure but damn fun to think about!

1970s

The progressive social values of the 1960s, such as increasing political awareness and the liberties of women, continued to accelerate during this new decade. Opposition to the Vietnam War, nuclear weapons, big business and government continued with the counterculture movement, which by this time was much more subdued. Area progress also continued, as projects such as the Broome County Veterans Memorial Arena, a 6,800-seat multipurpose arena in Binghamton, New York, was completed in 1973.

Local boxing contributors included Eddie Vick (1956–70), Tony Ventura (1966–74), Tommy Kost (1970–78), Jim Howard (1967–71), Dennis "Rocky" Cudney (1969–74), Hal "TNT" Carroll (1964–78), Billy Harris (coach, cornerman) and Angelo Prospero (author, historian).

When the 1974 Olympic Games took place in Montreal, Canada, Pat Nappi was coaching the boxing team—a group that captured five gold medals. He had begun his boxing instructional career in the United States Army over two decades earlier, and his skills had already landed him a position on the 1974 national AAU boxing team, which participated in the World Games in Cuba. As national boxing coach of the United States from 1974 to 1988, he was pivotal in the development of a new generation of quicker, smarter and stronger fighters. A perfect example was the 1984 Olympic boxing team. Coached by Pat Nappi, the group took home nine gold medals (Gonzales, McCrory, Taylor, Whitaker, Page, Brooklyn's Mark

Breland, Tate, Tillman and Biggs), one silver medal (Hill) and one bronze medal (Holyfield). Robert Shannon, who was eliminated in the second round, was the only boxer who did not medal. Upstate New York found a treasure in Pat Nappi.

1980s

Quiet social and economic change became the norm as wealth and production migrated to newly industrializing economies during the 1980s. Big fights had become national showcases destined for the glitter of Las Vegas or Atlantic City. The dynamics of the entertainment business also convinced the fight game that marketing away from minor markets might provide greater success—which it did. Construction continued, albeit education-related, as the Carrier Dome, a 49,250-seat domed sports stadium located on the campus of Syracuse University, was opened on September 20, 1980.

Boxing contributors of this decade include Vic Brown (1963–82), Greg Sorrentino (1976–83), Kevin Rooney (1979–85, also manager, trainer), Teddy Atlas (trainer) and Edward Brophy (executive director, IBHOF).

Growing up in the Kennedy Square section (east side) of Syracuse, southpaw Frankie Liles found his calling when he discovered boxing. He compiled an impressive amateur record while collecting a string of awards, including 1986 national Golden Gloves welterweight champion, 1987 United States amateur light middleweight champion and 1988 runner-up for the Olympic team at light middleweight (decisioned twice by Roy Jones Jr).

Liles began his professional career in Detroit at the famous Kronk Gym. He then headed west to Los Angeles to begin fighting and accumulating wins, while positioning himself for a title shot. He captured the North American super middleweight title by defeating Merqui Sosa on October 21, 1992. Liles then went on to capture the World Boxing Association super middleweight championship with a stunning decision over WBA champ Steve Little (1994-W12). That December, he defended his title against Michael Nunn (W12), followed by a win over Frederic Seillier (1995-KO6) and then a unanimous decision over Brazil's Mauricio Amaral (1995-W12). At this point, his impressive record stood at 28-1.

By his retirement from the ring in 1999, Frankie Liles had defended his super middleweight title numerous times and become a true champion—a tribute to his boxing skills, as well as to his manager, Jack O' Halloran, and trainers, Kenny Adams and Freddie Roach. Fabulous Frankie is so beloved in the city of Syracuse that Mayor Roy Bernardi declared a day in his honor.

Even as a kid, Ralph "Rocky" Fratto dreamed of being a professional boxer. Beginning his career in the service, he compiled an impressive amateur record of over fifty victories. Fratto then approached legendary trainer Tony Graziano, who had assisted many boxers, about managing his professional career. Coaxing Graziano, who had retired, would be no easy task, but Fratto was relentless, as was his father, Ralph Sr. Once his team was in place, Rocky reeled off more than twenty straight wins, drawing huge crowds all over Western and Central New York.

On April 25, 1981, before nine thousand boxing fans at Rochester's War Memorial, Rocky won the NABF middleweight title by decisioning Rocky Mosley. This gained him a WBA title shot for Sugar Ray Leonard's vacated crown against Japan's Tadashi Mihara on November 7, 1981, in Rochester. Fratto lost the close fifteen-round decision to Mihara in a hard-fought contest.

1990s

The later part of the twentieth century would reflect the "new media" decade, a marriage between digital and communication technology. Information was being converted into new forms. But many boxing records remained obscured and in deteriorating condition, such as old periodicals and newspapers. Extraction required patience and the painstaking adherence to preservation and conservation methods, all characteristics of a historian. In December 1984, Paul Zabala, of Saratoga Springs, joined the International Boxing Research Organization (IBRO) and became one of IBRO's most prolific researchers. His contributions, including *The Ring Record Book and Boxing Encyclopedia*, will be appreciated for decades.

Born in Tonawanda, New York, on November 27, 1973, Baby Joe Mesi captured the hearts of many Upstate boxing fans at the turn of the century. He began his professional career in 1997, working his way through the heavyweight ranks, battling at many popular Upstate facilities including the Pepsi Arena in Albany and the Turning Stone Casino in Verona. On September 17, 1999, he captured the New York State heavyweight title by defeating Anthony Green at the Flickenger Athletic Center in Buffalo (TKO8).

From this point forward, Mesi was a man on a mission, virtually undeniable. On June 24, 2003, he kayoed Robert Davis (TKO1) for the vacant NABF vacant heavyweight title. Mesi was not just beating the talent he faced, but he was also devouring it with his impressive arsenal of knockout punches. Then, on March 13, 2004, he beat Vassiliy Jirov at Mandalay Bay Resort & Casino in Las Vegas, Nevada. But Mesi's promising boxing career was greatly affected when he suffered at least two subdural hematomas (bleeding around the brain). The injuries resulted in his indefinite suspension by the Nevada Athletic Commission, which effectively banned him from boxing anywhere in the United States. His activity has since been limited.

2000 AND BEYOND: BOXING TODAY

As we enter a new century, the spirit of boxing remains strong in Central New York. The Albany City Boxing Program is a great example of just how forceful it is. This program teaches boys and girls instructional boxing techniques. It also teaches them discipline, while increasing their strength and flexibility. Under the tutelage of Director Vladimir Koshnitsky, there are two boxing program locations in the city of Albany: the Quail Street location, opened in March 2000 (this facility offers an after-school boxing program for children ages twelve to eighteen) and the Lincoln Park location.

Mayor Gerald D. Jennings and the City of Albany's Department of Recreation opened the new Youth Fitness Center at the Lincoln Park Bathhouse in April 2007. The Youth Fitness Center is a state-of-the-art fitness center that offers boxing, jump-roping, weight training, cardiovascular training and a dance fitness program. Open to boys and girls ages seven to nineteen, it is sewing the seeds of a new generation.

These programs have had their share of rising stars, but perhaps their greatest gift has been Quail Street boxing coach Jerrick Jones and what he means to Capital District boxing. For a decade, he has molded raw fighters not only into skilled boxers but also into fine young adults—not a simple task by any means.

If individually each of us is a single drop, then collectively we make up an ocean in the story of boxing—a talented pool of individuals whose origins can be traced to Upstate New York and whose reflections can be seen in the moniker "Title Town, USA."

4

Carmen Basilio

Road to Robinson

Carmen Basilio was born to Canastota sharecropper Joseph Basilio (1886–1974) and his wife, Mary Picciano (1893–1985), on April 2, 1927. He was preceded by Jessie, Lucy, Matilda, Anna, Nellie and Armando and followed by Paul, Delores and Joseph. Raising such a large family on Barlow Street was no easy task, but the Basilios, like so many others, persevered and made do with what they had—often a cherished memory or simply one another. Family traditions remained paramount, and recollections were treasured.

A stubborn yet determined Carmen Basilio learned early in life that he was going to have to work, and work hard. If Canastota's employment options weren't conducive to him, alternatives needed to be considered. His father, who was also Carmen's mentor, was a boxing fan and shared his interest in the sport with those who listened. Carmen listened—in fact, intently. He wanted more out of life than what he saw as his future. But getting from point A, the onion farms of Canastota, to point B, the championship of the world, required a path. The Marine Corps provided what would be the perfect springboard into the sport. It had areas of responsibilities that included things like "the development of tactics, technique and equipment"—all words familiar to a boxer. When he finished fighting for his country, he started fighting for himself professionally in 1948 at the age of twenty-one. The craggy-faced ex–onion farmer and ex-marine was now a boxer.

Today, the name Basilio evokes adjectives like "fearless" and "gritty" and figures of speech such as "tough as nails" or "eat leather." Naturally, fights are recalled from visitors, primarily the title bouts. Records, too, are

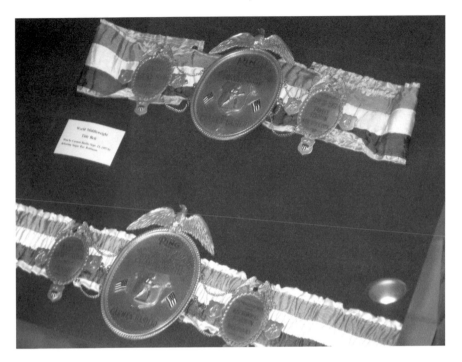

The Basilio championship belts rest safely inside the walls at 1 Hall of Fame Drive in Canastota, New York.

examined; the interest is always keen and the admiration respectful and unfailingly genuine. But since his retirement in 1961 and the birth of the International Boxing Hall of Fame twenty-eight years later, it seems that the most common inquiry has been the "Road to Robinson"—not only who, when and where he fought, but also, as Paul Harvey would say, "the rest of the story."

THE ROAD TO ROBINSON

Most ring historians would conclude that, pound for pound, Walker Smith Jr., born in Detroit on May 3, 1921, was the greatest fighter ever. The George Gainford description "Sweet as Sugar" defined his ring prowess. He was as graceful as he was undeniable. Unbeaten, untied and unscored-upon in his first forty fights, "Sugar" Ray Robinson personified his term of endearment.

When Basilio decided to turn pro, Robinson, with nearly ninety wins and only one loss, held the world welterweight title. He fought only five times in 1948 and won all five bouts. It was all he needed to do. Robinson was living in Harlem, where he was well known, accomplished, comfortable and tending to myriad problems, none of which were inside the ring.

1948

Democratic incumbent Harry S Truman defeated Republican Thomas E. Dewey. It was the fall of a leap year, and Basilio, after a few unrecorded "bootleg" battles, considered jumping into the ring professionally, which he did on November 24, 1948, against Auburn's Jimmy Evans in Binghamton, New York.

At five feet, six and a half inches tall and fighting in an orthodox stance, Basilio was primed to address his welterweight opponents—or so he thought. It was an auspicious beginning for the fighter, who found a measure of his marine ring skills in victories over his first four professional opponents: Evans, Williamsport's Bruce Walters, Philadelphia's Eddie Thomas and Albany's Rolly Johns. To be frank, Basilio liked the money for the job!

Like most, he would begin his professional career slowly, learning the ropes, not just climbing through them. Skills, tactics and training would all need to be refined. Let's face it: Kalurah Temple in Binghamton, New York, is long way from Madison Square Garden.

1949

After his first full year, Basilio was 15-2-2. He defeated target practice victim Ernie Hall, "tomato can" Luke Jordan, Cleveland fighter Jerry Drain, Dayton fighter Johnny Clemons, Baltimore journeyman Johnny Cunningham (twice), Buffalo fighter Jesse Bradshaw, Baltimore ring veteran Sammy Daniels, Buffalo's Tony DiPelino and Springfield's Jackie (Johnny) Parker. But he drew Johnny Cunningham (first of four battles) and Bronx journeyman Jimmy "Jay" Parlin and lost to Elma, New York fighter Connie Thies and to Cunningham. Nevertheless, his slow start was rectified, his knockout punch sharpened a bit and even the Thies loss proved a learning experience. As an environment, the fight world was still new.

Sugar Ray Robinson, now with over one hundred victories, found the highlight of 1949 to be his July rematch with Kid Gavilan. The fights leading up to "the Cuban Hawk" were referred to by Robinson's handlers as sparring sessions, although the draw with Buffalo's Henry Brimm was far from it. Robinson had fought the capable and scrappy Brimm the previous year to a decision victory in Buffalo at the Memorial Auditorium. Gavilan wanted to avenge his previous year's loss, and Robinson knew it, so he trained long and hard at Greenwood Lakes, New York. Robinson, who suffered a cut over the right eye in the fourth round, bled throughout the bout but eventually took the close-distance decision.

1950

Carmen Basilio, now 22-5-3, defeated Buffalo's "Sonny" Jim Hampton and Cleveland busher Cassill Tate and marinated Frenchman and former Johnny Saxton opponent Adrien Mourguiart (Mogart), veteran Lew Jenkins (his first "real" opponent), Montreal's Gaby "Frenchy" Ferland and Argentine Guillermo Giminez, twice. But Basilio drew Gaby "Frenchy" Ferland and lost to Pittsburgh fighter Mike Koballa, veteran Eddie Giosa and Hartford's southpaw Vic Cardell.

Regarding the "experience and nerves" losses, three things are worth noting. First, working in Koballa's corner that night, watching his fighter outbox Basilio, was a young Angelo Dundee. Second, as a light welterweight, Eddie Giosa had already met Bob Montgomery, Lew Jenkins, Beau Jack, Sandy Saddler, Ike Williams and Willie Pep. And third, the final fight of the year, with Cardell, was held in Madison Square Garden on December 15, 1950—Carmen Basilio's first visit to boxing's Mecca.

Meanwhile, "Sugar" Ray Robinson was in peak form and did not lose a single fight in 1950. He began the year with some tough confrontations stateside, including Ray Barnes, Robert Villemain (title bout), Charley Fusari (title bout), Jose Basora (title bout) and Bobo Olson (title bout). He and his entourage then headed to Europe, via the SS *Liberte*, to face some good opponents, including Luc Von Dam, Jean Walzack and Robert Villemain (rematch). The fight with the Dutchman van Dam was marred by a low blow, buttressing Robinson's reputation as a dirty fighter. Vacillating between boxing divisions means managing weight differences—not easy for any fighter, unless you are Robinson, of course. He finished the year at a career 120-1-2.

Robinson was also modifying his persona, lashing out against discrimination where and when he could, becoming more aware of being a role model to young boys, not only in Harlem, but also across America. He was "Sugar" being "Sugar," even trading in his dark blue Buick for an auspicious pink Cadillac.

1951

A low-frequency fight year, at a 50 percent winning percentage, does not bode well for any fighter. In fact, it is a bit humiliating. Basilio defeated three opponents in 1951: Cuban Flora Hita, Eddie Giosa and Cleveland veteran fighter Shamus McCray. But he also lost to three opponents: Detroit, Michigan's hard-hitting fighter Lester Felton (Syracuse), Hartford's Johnny Cesario (Utica) and Rochester's Ross Virgo (New Orleans).

In Basilio's defense, Felton entered the ring with over forty wins, having beaten some solid fighters, including a controversial victory over Kid Gavilan and a decision over Bobby Dykes. Cesario was a talented fighter who had amassed a thirty-seven-consecutive-victory streak during his career and also held the New England welterweight and middleweight titles. And yes, Syracuse fight fans, that is the same Ross Virgo who put Rolly Johns to the canvas five times at the State Fair Coliseum only a couple years earlier (1949). (OK, I may be reaching with that last one. Perhaps it would be better to say be careful where you fight.)

During the 1950s, if one scans the print—especially the commentary by the few respected writers, such as Dan Parker at the *New York Daily Mirror* or Jimmy Cannon at the *Post*—one could easily suspect that the fight game was dirty. Claims by some that Jewish and Italian mobsters had hooks at all levels were disturbing but not at all surprising. Gambling and corruption had followed professional sports for decades. Senator Estes Kefauver and John Gurnee Bonomi mounted a crusade in hopes of instigating boxing reform, but at what price and when?

As for Mr. Robinson, he put together another solid year, picking up the world middleweight title from Jake LaMotta (1951-KO13), who had won the belt from Marcel Cerdan. During the "St. Valentine's Day Massacre," Robinson sliced and diced for seven rounds but never toe-to-toe against LaMotta. This was a prelude to an unmerciful battering of the bull. The thirteenth round of the fight, considered by many historians to be one of the greatest rounds in fight history, was merciless.

Robinson then lost the belt to a talented Randy Turpin (1951-L15) in London before regaining it in a rematch only a couple months later (KO-10) in New York. The highly anticipated September 12 rematch, held at the Polo Grounds, attracted more than sixty-one thousand spectators. Robinson, with a gash over his left eye and blood running down his face, conducted a clinic in the tenth and forced referee Ruby Goldstein to stop the damage to Turpin. Many historians consider the Turpin rematch Robinson's finest moment.

Originally the Onondaga War Memorial, this arena hosted many Basilio battles in downtown Syracuse, New York.

There would be joy again in Harlem, like there was when Joe Louis knocked out Max Schmeling in 1938 and like there always was when Sugar returned home. His café was a mere thirty blocks from the Polo Grounds. Robinson, with nearly 130 career wins and only 2 losses, appeared invincible. At this point, Basilio had more losses in 1951 than Robinson had in his entire career.

1952

The year, a seventy-six-round education, proved bittersweet for Basilio, who finished at a career 31-10-4. He defeated Pennsylvania fighter Emmett Norris, Akron's Jimmy Cousins, Connecticut's Jackie O'Brien (his first fight against a former DeMarco opponent), Cuban Baby Williams, Connecticut's Sammy Giuliani and Omaha's Chuck Foster. But he drew Michigan southpaw Chuck Davey before losing to him in a rematch, followed by a loss to Billy Graham. It was the third consecutive year with back-to-back losses for the Canastota fighter.

In advocacy of Basilio, the much-anticipated ten rounder against the undefeated Davey (32-0-1) at the Syracuse War Memorial Auditorium on May 29 turned out to be a fiasco. Refereed by Joe Palmer, the fight was originally called a victory for Basilio. It was then switched to a draw when a couple of errors were found on one of the judges' score cards. Both fight camps were furious and demanded a rematch, which they got on July 16. Simply stated, in the second Davey match, Basilio—in his first televised bout—was out of place, out of step and outpointed.

Also, veteran Billy Graham, with nearly one hundred career wins, was a quick and masterful fighter who would never be knocked off his feet—not by Basilio, not by anyone. The caliber of soldiers entering the ring against Basilio had improved, as had the politics outside it.

The year's high point, from this point forward, was the fighter's association with Angelo Dundee, whom he used in Miami Beach during the Williams fight. Basilio, complaining that promoter Chris Dundee was "too damn cheap to give him enough airline tickets," now found himself looking for a trainer. In stepped Dundee's brother Angelo, who would prove much more than just a bucket jockey. "I always wrapped my own hands," Carmen recalled, "never trusted anybody else—even had my own bag."

According to Angelo Dundee, "Carmen told me to 'wrap 'em,' so I wrapped 'em, and I hadn't done it since Chickie [Ferrara] told me to do it [referring to a different fight]." Not only did Basilio approve of the tape job, but he also approved of his performance in the ring. As for Angelo—welcome aboard!

Sugar Ray Robinson fought only three times in 1952, but all were title bouts: Carl "Bobo" Olson (1952-W15), Rocky Graziano (1952-KO3) and Joey Maxim (1952-KO by 14). In the first defense of his second title reign, Robinson defeated Olson in a mundane middleweight bout. But the Graziano fight was much different—a highly anticipated contest

The boxing license of Angelo Dundee, hall of fame trainer to Carmen Basilio.

between two thirty-year-old sluggers. Although Robinson was floored in the third round, Graziano's aggressive middleweight style and leading chin proved to be an easy target. He was knocked out in the third. The last fight of the year, an attempt by Robinson to "move up" against light heavyweight champion Joey Maxim, was held at Yankee Stadium. Adverse conditions—rain, a ringside temperature of 105 degrees and a somewhat stationary Maxim—proved to be too much for Robinson. In the first and only time a fight of his was stopped on his account, Ray couldn't answer the fourteenth-round bell. By now a successful businessman, Robinson would announce his retirement in December 1952, thereby giving up his middleweight title. At 131-2-2, he concluded this phase of his career.

The scramble for the middleweight belt had begun!

1953

Eight days before Dwight D. Eisenhower succeeded Harry S Truman as president of the United States, Carmen Basilio began a new year facing his most talented opponent to date—Ike Williams. Having won the NBA world title by defeating Juan Zurita in April 1945, Williams, with his terrific right hand, had captured the attention of many around the fight game. He held the crown until May 1951, when he was stopped by Jimmy Carter. With over one hundred career victories, the Brunswick, Georgia fighter was at the tail end of a brilliant career. He was so gifted a boxer that he would make any historian's list of the one hundred greatest punchers of all time.

Williams, in his last fight—a seven-round TKO victory over local fighter Pat Manzi at the Syracuse War Memorial Auditorium—seemed to have shed some holiday ring rust. But he had lost three of his last five fights, prompting critics to cast aspersions toward him and his handlers. Since vindication for Manzi's loss was overdue, at least in the eyes of area fight fans, anticipation was high for Williams's return to Syracuse. True to form, if Basilio was intimidated in any fashion, he certainly didn't show it. The fight went the ten-round distance, and the unanimous decision was awarded to Basilio.

As for Williams, well, once he learned he couldn't manage himself—a decision he had recently made— he was blackballed by the boxing managers guild and had little choice but to allow a clandestine Blinky Palermo handle his affairs. Both of these latter elements clearly controlled the sport. Williams was now another chess piece on the fight-game checkerboard.

The Basilio camp then moved west, on February 28, and avenged his 1950 loss to Hartford's Vic Cardell (Toledo, Ohio) before heading home on April 11 to knock out the Brooklyn-born Carmine Fiore.

With the summer heat came a double dose of Billy Graham, who was an enigma to many—profound balance with little passion for the knockout. Now at the end of a hall of fame career with one hundred ring victories, Graham would tangle again with Basilio, but this time in Syracuse on June 6—a volatile mix from any perspective. It was doubtful that either fighter would end up kissing the canvas, and both were almost certain to go the distance. It was, however, Basilio's first twelve-round fight. When it was over, the decision was unanimous: the New York State welterweight title now belonged to Carmen Basilio.

Their second battle of the year came shortly after, on July 25. At this point in his career, Graham had never lost back-to-back fights against the same opponent. But neither had Basilio; the closest were the fights with Chuck Davey. The excitement in Syracuse was commensurate with any Basilio bout to-date, but so was the concern. How would Basilio fare in another twelve-round fight? What impact would a new referee—Petey Scalzo—have on the decision? On this day, in this arena—the War Memorial Auditorium—this fight was determined a draw based on the only even score card, that of the sole judge to score both Graham fights, Jack Michaels. As one might imagine, such an anticlimactic ending to such a good fight trilogy was a stroke of bathos.

On September 18, in his fiftieth fight, Carmen Basilio got his first world championship shot—a fifteen-round battle for the world welterweight title at the War Memorial Auditorium in Syracuse. His opponent was Gerardo Gonzalez, better known as "Kid" Gavilan. The hard-hitting Gavilan captured the title in 1951 by beating Johnny Bratton in a fifteen-round decision. He then successfully—all right, creatively— defended it against the likes of Bobby Dykes, Gil Turner and Billy Graham. Credited with inventing the bolo punch, Gavilan was crafty and colorful, the perfect opponent to pack seven thousand fans inside the War Memorial Auditorium. Basilio, a 4-1 underdog, entered the ring at 147 pounds—a quarter-pound advantage. In the second round, Basilio sent Gavilan to the canvas with two sharp left hooks. Regaining his composure after a nine count, Gavilan got up and continued fighting. Despite suffering a nosebleed and being unable to put away the champion, Basilio remained confident and fought well into the ninth round.

As the final round began, most had the fight even. Both fighters continued relying on their lefts, as other aspects of their arsenals seemed ineffective. When the imported judges' score cards were announced, the partisan audience was stunned. The implausible had happened—Gavilan was victorious. Basilio was beside himself, rebuffing attempts to console him. The crowd was incensed, perplexed and crying foul.

Still livid over the Gavilan fight, Basilio then knocked out the familiar Johnny Cunningham and drew Frenchman Pierre Langlois. A pivotal twelve months in the career of Carmen Basilio ended as eight fights concluded in five wins, one loss and two draws. Three title fights, totaling thirty-nine rounds of an eighty-two-round year, were concluded. Was it the path of

Kid Gavilan, "the Cuban Hawk," autographs a boxing glove on the grounds of the International Boxing Hall of Fame.

opportunity for the Canastota fight artist? Only time would tell. Gavilan, who showed minimal vulnerability both inside and outside the ring, moved on to retain his title against the familiar Johnny Bratton.

Ever since announcing his retirement from the ring, Ray Robinson had been restless. His various businesses proved challenging but were no replacement for the sport he loved. Living only a stone's throw from Broadway (Riverdale), he caught the theatre bug and utilized his other skill—dancing. Naturally, two entertainment careers in one family (his wife, Edna Mae, was a dancer and model) proved challenging. For Ray, every turn continued to be a provocation—and not a three-minute one.

1954

On January 16, two days after Marilyn Monroe married baseball player Joe DiMaggio, Carmen and company headed to Miami, Florida, home of the Fifth Street Gym. There, in a typical Basilio slow start to the year, he drew Italian welterweight champ Italo Scortichini. He then went on to defeat Pierre Langlois in a second match, Scortichini in a rematch, Minnesota fighter Al Andrews, West Virginia's journeyman Ronnie Harper twice, Brooklyn's Carmine Fiore and solid Detroit fighter Allie Gronik. Carmen Basilio was now 43-11-7, with seven consecutive wins, and hadn't lost a fight since September 1953.

Comparatively speaking, after sixty-one fights, Sugar Ray Robinson had a record of 59-1-1. But Basilio was fighting at a different time and out of a different place. Robinson had the comfort of the big city and a prewar attitude. He was twenty-four years old then, three years younger than the hungry Basilio at the end of 1954. The attitudes and politics had changed, but discipline, which had been driven into Basilio throughout his adolescence and by the Marine Corps, had not.

The Gavilan loss was behind him, and the memory of the last three draws was fading. Basilio's fine-tuning was approaching perfection. Clearly a contender for the welterweight crown, the Basilio camp would weigh its options over the months ahead. Positioning its fighter would be everything—but how?

Ray Robinson was not an astute businessman, nor was he an entertainment legend—outside the ring, that is—but he was nobody's fool either. Mortgage foreclosures, unpaid taxes and dwindling assets were all part of Ray's undercard, so to speak. His only option was to wipe the slate clean by coming out of retirement. It would be a quiet reemergence on November 29, 1954, when Ray starting shaking off the ring rust in an exhibition against stablemate Gene Burton.

1955

Two weeks after Marian Anderson became the first African American singer to perform at the Metropolitan Opera in New York City, Carmen Basilio took on Peter Mueller in Syracuse. A victory over the tough German middleweight champion would be a great start for Basilio—and that's exactly what happened.

Leonardo Liotta was born to Sicilian parents in Boston and lived in the city's ethnic North End community. Unable to fight at the age of sixteen, he used the birth certificate of Tony DeMarco to begin his professional career—a technique used by many fighters, including Ray Robinson. Having surprisingly upset Johnny Saxton for the world welterweight crown on April 1, 1955 (KO-14), DeMarco had to face Basilio within ninety days.

The June 10 stage seemed set for Basilio: he was the top-ranked contender, with eight consecutive victories; the fight was at the War Memorial Auditorium, his hometown; and the partisan fans knew only one North End, and that was on Salina Street in Syracuse. It was a prescription for a knockout to some, but most knew that DeMarco was a machine inside the ring. His disposal of Syracuse's Pat Manzi in the first round in their battle in Boston (1954-KO1) was an undeniable pronouncement.

The gladiators were evenly matched toe-to-toe sluggers and aggressive battlers, making the outcome uncertain. By the eighth round, DeMarco, hands low and with a cut over his right eye, took some Basilio uppercuts and then a solid right and fell to the canvas. He was down again before the bell conveniently sounded. Following an eleventh-round physician's visit to DeMarco's corner, the bell sounded and the fight continued. In enduring, rather than boxing, energy is expelled only as needed by both fighters. By the twelfth round, DeMarco was dead on his feet. Although he caught Basilio during some careless moments, it was clear that the well had run dry. Before DeMarco could get hurt, referee Harry Kessler stopped the battle at 1:52 in the twelfth round. The new world welterweight champion was Carmen Basilio.

In keeping with the Italian theme, Basilio was back in the ring on August 10 to battle Italo Scortichini. He disposed of his Madison Square Garden opponent in a ten-round unanimous decision. Philadelphia contender Gil Turner, clearly in the welter title mix, was next (September 7). In a tough encounter that some felt ended in a draw, the hometown decision—which was supported by referee Ruby Goldstein's card—went to Basilio.

Basilio v. DeMarco II took place on November 30 at the Boston Garden in Boston, Massachusetts. It seemed like the entire North End of the city had shown up to watch hometown favorite DeMarco avenge his loss. Both fighters, armed with fight-ending left hooks, entered the ring weighing an identical 145½ pounds. Style, stamina and strategy—all reexamined or reconfirmed following the first fight—would determine the outcome. Basilio would start inside low and try to punch up, while DeMarco would try to time the assault to land a powerful right counter.

An upright DeMarco landed a few good parries during the first round but, similar to the first fight, had trouble measuring and connecting with his bigger punches. To shouts of "Cut him up Tony, cut him up!" both fighters entered round two, and it wasn't long before blood was seen over DeMarco's left eye. By the third round, Basilio had improved his defense against DeMarco's right, which was connecting a bit earlier. Meanwhile, DeMarco was coming in lower on assaults in hopes of improved accuracy. But when DeMarco got Basilio against the ropes, he failed to keep him there long enough to do any damage. A few wild DeMarco hooks also missed their mark.

In round four, DeMarco staggered Basilio with a solid left hook but couldn't capitalize. He also opened a slight cut over Basilio's right eye. It was the first three-minute cycle when fatigue was clearly noticeable in both fighters. The fifth round belonged to DeMarco, who landed some solid combinations, complemented by some good left hooks, but the sixth was little more than a sparring session.

Basilio came out more aggressive in the seventh but took some good left jabs from DeMarco. Although the Boston boxer had some unattractive flat-footed misses, he was able to stagger Basilio with a powerful left hook. An unstable Basilio then managed to fight on instinct to finish the round. Sensing that the momentum was in his favor, DeMarco catapulted forward in the next round and landed a solid right, but Basilio managed to shake it off. DeMarco looked steady but would slow in the lackluster ninth.

Both fighters decided to go inside during the tenth, landing a few good combinations but inflicting no real damage. With fatigue mounting, both fighters locked up whenever possible. Trading punches in the eleventh, DeMarco failed to back Basilio into a corner—an opportunity missed or just a failure of execution? Momentum now favored Basilio, who roared back in the twelfth round with a tremendous array of combinations. The devastation found DeMarco falling helplessly into the corner. Up at an eight count, Basilio attacked and fired DeMarco face-first into the canvas. The bout was stopped at 1:54 in the twelfth round, giving Basilio the TKO. The acknowledged fight of the year by multiple sources was a mere two seconds longer than the first meeting.

Tony DeMarco would go on to embellish his legacy in Boston's rich sports history. Next time you're in the city's North End, look for Tony DeMarco Way. The talented fighter also put four straight wins together after this loss—Wallace (Bud) Smith, Arthur Persley, Vince Martinez and Kid Gavilan—before succumbing to Gaspar Ortega in two out of three consecutive fights. Finishing his career at 58-12-1, DeMarco retired in 1962.

Carmen Basilio was the 1955 Fighter of the Year, as named by nearly every respected boxing source. With that said, let's spend a few seconds on a second.

"You're only as good as the fighter you work with." This claim, attributed to corner legend Ray Arcel, could certainly apply to Angelo Dundee. He trained his first world champion in Carmen Basilio. This unique "blend"—so to speak—of an Upstate onion farmer with a downstate bucket guy was as perfect as an autumn Adirondack amble.

Apprenticing in the late 1940s and early 1950s, Dundee kept his mouth shut and observed everything, every detail. New York City was the Mecca of boxing, and Stillman's Gym was the home of its prophets— or "profits," depending on your perspective. Working out of his brother Chris's office in the Capitol Hotel was convenient. It was catty-corner to the old Garden at Fifty-first and Eighth Avenue and a bucket toss from the Ringside Cafeteria. He learned from the best: Ray Arcel, Chickie Ferrara and Charley Goldman, as much over a cup a coffee at the Ringside as up the street on Eighth Avenue at Stillman's.

The trainer befriended Charley Goldman, the former bantam who trained heavyweight Rocky Marciano. Goldman taught Dundee not to alter a fighter's natural skills, a strategy that Dundee followed with Basilio. He also taught him the principles of size—if you are small or tall, stay that way—a lesson that would prove worthy of a belt for Basilio.

Dundee's observations were keen, his strategies consistent and his routine often flawless. From sizing up an arena on the night of a fight to wrapping a fighter's hands, familiarity bred comfort. Unfamiliarity with detail became his nemesis. During a fight, he blocked out the confusion and concentrated on the fighter, not instructing on the obvious but on what the fighter was lacking in detail. What was he failing to accomplish and why? Dundee, while appreciating strength, preferred technique; time and time again, his catch phrase was repeated: "Nice and easy."

The gifted trainer also picked up a bag of tricks along the way, and like anyone in his position, he would use them on an as-needed basis. Most of us would later become familiar with a few—such as his small tear in Ali's glove during the Henry Cooper fight—but there were others. It's not bending the rules or cheating, but simply applying them to one's benefit. Dundee was a Basilio benefactor, as were managers Johnny DeJohn or Joe Netro. In conjunction, they were an incontestable quartet.

Sugar Ray Robinson was now back in the fight game, disposing first of the flat-nosed ex-marine from Roxbury, Massachusetts, Joe Rindone. Having brought new sparring partners into his stable, with the goal of preparing him for both Fullmer—whom he would fight twice before Basilio (1957–L15 and KO5)—and Basilio, Robinson was too busy thinking about the title to think about his next fight, against Ralph "Tiger" Jones. The boxer ripped into Robinson like a jackal and left him barely standing. The loss devastated everyone around Robinson, and uncertainty abounded. A lackluster split decision against Johnny Lombardo followed; the victory was hardly worth a celebration. Robinson's quickness wasn't back, and neither was his snappy jab or his confidence in his handlers, who contemplated calling off the comeback. Next, he disposed of an overmatched Ted Olla before a birthday victory over Garth Panter.

The march toward the championship heated up in July with a decision victory over Rocky Castellani. Then a right uppercut, with a finishing left hook, sent reigning champion Bobo Olson to the canvas in the second round of their December title fight in Chicago. The middleweight title again belonged to Robinson, who was now holding it for the third time.

1956

On March 14, the day after the King released what would be his first gold album—his self-titled *Elvis Presley*—the city of Chicago welcomed two great combatants. In the first meeting of what would become a classic ring trilogy, the new titleholder, Basilio, stepped out against Jersey fighter Johnny Saxton. Turning professional in 1949, Saxton compiled over thirty-five wins before losing to Gil Turner in 1953. His quest for the world welterweight championship came into focus once he defeated both Joey Giardello (1953) and Johnny Bratton (1954). The next issue, not so simple, was getting a 1954 title shot at Kid Gavilan. Then, in the blink (as in Frank "Blinky" Palermo) of an eye—or for the "Money Honey," as Elvis would say—there was Gavilan. On October 20, 1954, in a fight that saw more action at the concession stand than in the ring, Saxton slipped away with a fifteen-round decision in Philadelphia. It was a fight between two boxers completely in control—sort of.

On April Fools' Day 1955, in his first defense of the championship, Saxton was bulldozed by hometown favorite Tony DeMarco in fourteen rounds. A raucous, albeit slightly partisan, crowd of nearly nine thousand Bostonians watched underdog DeMarco send Saxton to never-never land with his trademark left hook. Delivered as sweetly as a Ted Williams line drive at Fenway, the punch was as utopian as it was propitious.

Countering the loss with some soft-pedal victories led to a fifteen-round title contest with Basilio slated for Chicago Stadium. Beginning when Saxton's handlers cut his glove—conveniently after a series of solid blows—the bout reeked of foul play. But nobody—I mean nobody—would be prepared for the outcome. When the unanimous decision was given to "the Fighting Orphan," an enraged crowd clamored for justice. To quote from Elvis's album for the last time, it was a "One-Sided Love Affair." Basilio was incensed, and as one fan put it, "had the fight been in Syracuse, the judges would be hanging in Clinton Square."

Local promoter Norm Rothschild and the Arena Boxing Club, along with James D. Norris and crew, were tapped for the September 12 rematch in Syracuse. The excitement began with the War Memorial Auditorium ring announcements from tenor Nick Tobin, who introduced the guests at the night's fight:

> *Here is the new lightweight champion from New Orleans, Joe E. Brown...And here's the leading contender for the middleweight crown from Buffalo, New York, Joey Giambra...And here's the new lightweight sensation from Marlborough, Connecticut, Larry Portland...And top contender for welterweight honors from Stamford, Connecticut, Chico Vejar...Here's the retired, undefeated heavyweight champion of the world...Come on up Rocky Marciano.*

Cheers went up from every section of the arena following the Brockton fighter's ring entrance. Rocco Francis Marchegiano was a ring apostle, idolized in Central New York and a household name across America. He was a fighter who was told he was too short, too light and lacked the reach to compete against the leading contenders.

When the opening bell rang, Saxton came out of his corner and brought a change in wardrobe, a new style, for a different dance—a slow dance inside and tight. Anticipating the all-too-familiar jab-and-counter approach from Saxton, Basilio seemed confused and looked to his corner for direction. A flat-footed Saxton had reversed his strategy and appeared as if he was going to try to punch it out with Basilio—a very risky alternative. Carmen's early round movement was quick, staying inside, out of range of solid contact, and rotating rounds between heavy body punches and headshots.

The Basilio camp would choose to wear down the 145¾-pound Saxton, who, as the fight progressed, felt less and less confident that the toe-to-toe decision made sense. Basilio's left hooks to the body and head were scoring, and a deep gash appeared on Saxton's lip. The fight was stopped in a ninth-round TKO at 1:31 by referee Al Berl. The fight of the year was over; the tables had been turned. It was an unmistakable outcome. Carmen Basilio finished the year 49-12-7.

Also in a two-fight year, Sugar Ray Robinson boxed all of fourteen rounds, four of which were spent retaining his title in a rematch against Carl "Bobo" Olson; the other ten were against journeyman Bob Provizzi. Robinson's business issues with the International Boxing Club (IBC) continued in 1956. He still blamed them for not getting a middleweight title shot in the mid-1940s. Concerns such as ticket allotments, fight times and even fight locations were a source of dissatisfaction. The organization, whose strings included exclusive leases such as Yankee Stadium, St. Nicholas Arena, etc., also included the seamless and inexplicable movement of fighters. These are the concerns of an experienced fighter, fully confident of his ability inside the ring but preoccupied with his affairs outside of it. While Robinson was a skilled negotiator, he was also an incompetent businessman.

1957

In a spring that saw Dr. Seuss's classic *The Cat in the Hat* published, the city of Cleveland was about to witness "the cat being let out of the bag," as a winner would finally be decided in a classic ring trilogy. A leaner, quicker and cocky Saxton had been training since December 10, confident that a return to his old style would prove victorious on February 22. He admitted that his decision in Syracuse "to fight Basilio's fight" and not his own was wrong.

Basilio, with a bruised right hand, which forced the postponement from the original fight date of January 18, had been training primarily out of Miami. Basilio's managers, Johnny DeJohn and Joe Netro, were optimistic but not overconfident. They brushed off questions like routine jabs. Basilio stayed reaffirmed— "I'll outbox him!"

Five crushing rights to Saxton's head scored their target in the first round, as inside body punching—a Basilio hallmark—began to inflict damage. Saxton was a toy in the second, battered from rope to rope at will. Saxton's eyes were glazed and his body was clearly on auxiliary power at this point. Basilio's left hook found the bottom of Saxton's jaw, and it was lights out. The fighter fell to his back, totally unconscious. After somehow finding the strength to lift himself up, the count continued—although the roar of the crowd was so loud that no number could be made out. The staggering fighter, looking for any sign of life in his legs, saw referee Tony LaBranch signal and stop the fight after 342 seconds. Afterward, a pensive Basilio was caught sitting alone in his dressing room, peeling an orange methodically and chanting to a three-syllable pulse: "Rob-in-son, Rob-in-son."

The Canastota camp then headed west to Portland to face ring veteran Harold Jones on May 16. The southpaw was recognized by Syracuse fight fans, many having seen a younger "Baby Face" box at MacArthur Stadium against Rochester's Harry Smith (1947) or in appearances at the State Fair Coliseum against Buffalo's Tommy Stenhouse (1948), Detroit's Mickey Savage (1948) or Buffalo's John Chatmon (1948). Referee Eddie Volk stopped the fight at 1:56 in the fourth round, giving the knockout to Basilio.

THE FIGHT

My boyhood dream was to win a championship in Yankee Stadium.
—Carmen Basilio

The pre-fight hype abounded, with boxing critics worldwide expressing their fight strategies and predictions about the September 23 bout. Most centered on the obvious differences between the fighters: height, weight and style. Few addressed heart. Perhaps it was Mark Twain who said it best when he crooned, "It's not the size of the dog in the fight, it's the size of the fight in the dog."

Basilio, clearly the smaller of the two, must stay close and work the body with short, quick and hard combinations; be alert to Robinson's powerful long hook; counter long hooks with inside body punches; get inside at the

Sculptor Earl Durand's statue of Carmen Basilio greets visitors inside the International Boxing Hall of Fame.

proper angle to block a right-side assault; keep his right shoulder up and in position to protect his chin; and inflict damage with his left hook. He could not allow his opponent punching room.

Robinson had to be patient with Basilio's low crouch; leverage the strength in his lower body; take full advantage of his height; and avoid Basilio's body blows with his quickness. He could not expose his deadly left or long right too soon or get frustrated with his target. Precision range meant maximum impact—a Robinson hallmark. Basilio would likely "fight up" the fighter, and Robinson was prepared to parry the assault. His two-fight prelude with Gene Fullmer, he thought, was enough preparation.

Basilio had been snubbed once by Robinson, and he never forgot it. His feelings toward the middleweight were firmly rooted, and he became transfixed on making him pay. Those who know Basilio, those who witnessed the fight and those who have talked to him in the years since understand how deeply Robinson had cut and how much Basilio despised the fighter.

The logistics for the Yankee Stadium fight were classic Robinson v. IBC. Daily threats from both sides filled the papers, and a "cancellation" was always imminent. While the IRS was a distraction due to Robinson's back taxes, the commission and promoter Jim Norris became the opposition, not Basilio. This diversion benefited the Canastota hopeful. Once the dust settled, the fighters' purses were as follows: Robinson, 45 percent of the gate, plus 45 percent of radio, movie and television receipts at a guaranteed $255,000; Basilio, 20 percent of the gate, plus 20 percent of radio, movie and television receipts at a guaranteed $110,000.

Patience—or was it cautious contempt—permeated the Basilio crew holding training camp up in Alexandria Bay, New York. The intensity was high, the fight films warm and the crisp clear water of the beautiful St. Lawrence River a nice diversion. There was plenty of bass and pike fishing. When a hook wasn't dropped in the water or thrown in the ring, one was used to entice another poker player to a few more rounds.

As for Robinson, training at the Harlem gym appeared as routine as his steady stream of business problems. He figured Basilio, at 51-12-7, would be weighing in at about the 151-pound level (Basilio weighed in at $153\frac{1}{2}$), thereby giving him the distinct advantage of nine pounds in weight and four and a half inches in height. This, accompanied by experience, would be enough to put away Basilio—or so he thought.

Since Carmen was always a Yankees fan, getting the team's dressing room was a critical fight logistic. Many of the players, including Casey Stengel and Billy Martin, stopped by to wish him well. Even Mickey Mantle, a fellow tenant farmer's son, greeted him prior to the bout.

It was a chilly Monday evening—fight night in New York—as the rich and famous assembled at or near ringside. From DiMaggio to Hemingway, it was a who's who of who was and even who wanted to be. Robinson opened, as he always did, with his machine-gun left jabs, measuring his opponent. Basilio immediately began executing his fight plan, getting by the barrage of left jabs, inside, ever inside, toward the body and up.

An uppercut bloodied Basilio's nose in the third, and a subsequent punch followed in the fourth, cutting his left eye. Like a demolition derby driver, Basilio took the damage in stride, relying on his cornerman Angelo Dundee "to polish, pinch 'em, patch 'em or paint 'em." By the fifth, Basilio's persistence was beginning to bond. He was no longer facing an insurmountable ring deity but a mortal thirty-seven-year-old man. With his ring pulchritude diminished, Robinson couldn't gainsay the will of Basilio.

In the sixth, Robinson managed to land an assault of timely jabs solidly on Basilio's face, but this did little to deter the Canastotan's fortitude. Robinson's fatigue started showing in the seventh; he was using his ring composure to steal needed minutes where and when he could. Hiding behind the left jabs, doing whatever was necessary to stop Basilio's sweeping rights and damaging left hooks, Robinson's frustration was evident.

By the eighth, a Dundee "quick lube" clearly painted Basilio's visage— protecting that eye was of prime importance. His plan still intact, Basilio went to the body and then to the head. The proposition was working. Robinson's trademark end-of-the-round flurry of punches, meant to impress the judges, continued, but it was now looking more and more like a desperation tactic.

Robinson went for a bike ride in both the ninth and tenth—anything to avoid a Basilio body barrage. Energy conservation was paramount and tactical planning a necessity. But was there enough time? The attack came in the eleventh, when Robinson besieged his opponent, pouring rights and lefts into his body. But it did not last. With sixty seconds left in the round, Basilio countered and, with three machine-gun rights to Robinson's jaw, sent him into the ropes. There, he unleashed a jackhammer assault to the head that looked like it might send Robinson to the canvas, but it did not. It was the ephemeral attack denied by the aegis of time; he came off the ropes just before the bell.

In the twelfth, after two lefts and a right to Basilio's head, Robinson was back in focus. Basilio's legs weakened; he staggered a bit but didn't fall. Robinson, dumbfounded by his opponent's quiddities, marveled at his resilience. How could this man, he thought, continue to endure?

Robinson pounded Basilio's face through the final rounds, and every time it looked like the fight was going his way, the tide shifted, and he took an onslaught from his opponent. Basilio would give no ground. The bell rang, and the fight was over.

Basilio had successfully transformed himself into a three-minute machine— tough not brilliant, determined but not predestined. A tactical error early in the fight had cost him; he had decided to fight from an upright stance rather than a crouch to avoid the Robinson uppercut. The excessive damage Basilio endured led back to his natural bobbing-and-weaving style—a change that may have won him the fight. The shift was immediately effective as Robinson's punches began missing their mark. Everyone knew how hard it was for a taller fighter to fight down on a vicious opponent, but Robinson was not just any tall fighter—he was the best pound for pound. Certainly he, of any fighter, could do it. Robinson's flurries were magnificent, but they weren't squalls and they needed to be. The post-fight anticipation was felt in the gut of all thirty-five thousand fans as the ring announcement was made:

> *Judge Ait Aadi scores it 9-5-1 even, Basilio. Referee Al Berl scores it 9 to 6, Robinson. The other judge, Bill Recht, scores it 8-6-1 even. The winner and new middleweight champion of the world: Carmen Basilio.*

At this hour, for one brief moment, every child who ever wanted to become a champion wanted to be Carmen Basilio.

UPSTATE NEW YORK

Most Controversial Ring Battles I

Buffalo	Dec. 20, 1895	Young Griffo v. Frank Erne	D4	A four round exhibition !
Utica	July 4, 1912	Jimmie Dragin v. George Newson	KO2	Newson dies after KO!
Albany	June 30, 1913	Willie Langford v. Kid Henry	NC	Dirty fight leads to a riot!
Syracuse	Jan. 20, 1919	Young Fisher v. Harry Greb	ND10	Fisher bites Greb at the Grand Opera House!
Utica	July 17, 1931	Bushy Graham v. Emil Paluso	KO8	Dirty fight at Convention Center!
Buffalo	April 2, 1946	Joe Matisi v. Dave Mason	KO3	Mason dies after KO!

Selected entries

5

Billy Backus

Mission: "Mantequilla"

W hen I first saw Billy Backus, he was outside of my gym fighting some kid," recalls Tony Graziano. "You know, an after school brawl, the kind we all had when we were young." Born on March 5, 1943, in Canastota, New York, Howard William "Billy" Backus was a tough kid, a southpaw scrapper with a bit of an edge and an attitude. Blessed with an athletic build, he quickly took a liking to sports. In high school, he played football and wrestled. He even wrestled with the general concept of high school; Backus withdrew briefly from formal education only to return in 1965 to meet graduation requirements. "'Hey kid, you wanna fight? Come up to my gym,'" Graziano recalls saying to him. "So he starts hanging out…I needed a sparring partner for one of my fighters, so I threw Billy into the mix."

So how did the genealogy surface, you ask? "I was outside the bank one day, and Nellie, Carmen Basilio's sister, strolls over and says, 'Hey, you got my kid boxing,'" Graziano admits with a smirk. And that's how the trainer learned more about his new addition.

With a former world champion for an uncle, one might assume that that would be enough impetus to look inside a ring for options, but there were more. Both fighters shared a passion; they liked to box, and they were good at it. Pressed by local employment options and blessed by good genetics, pugilism became a viable alternative. "He started holding his own while sparring," recalls Graziano, "becoming a good fighter. He could take a punch, had a tough chin…a punching little bastard."

"At age eighteen, we started working him up," states manager Graziano. "Usual way…went to other people's backyard to fight." Topped off, Backus fought at five feet, eight inches and at a weight range of between 143 and 151 pounds. His handsome, chiseled looks accentuated by razor-sharp sideburns were trendy and overt. As an amateur, his first match came at nearby Marion Manor in 1958; it was one of thirteen victories matched against only two losses. His potential became clear when he captured the Adirondack AAU featherweight title twice and reached the semifinals of the 1961 Nationals in Pocatello, Idaho. "He broke a lot of bags in the gym," Graziano affirms. "A tough, tough puncher."

FROM THE BEGINNING: 1962–1963

It would be an inauspicious beginning for Billy Backus. Tallying up fights in *The Ring Record Book* puts him at a record of 3-4-3 at the end of his tenth professional fight. In sixty rounds of professional boxing, all of his fights went the distance. The contrast between the lackluster records of those he defeated and the impressive records of those who beat him was immense. Although he wasn't stepping up to the competition, Backus was boxing—even if the painting on the canvas was far from pretty.

The comparisons to his uncle—Basilio was 8-0-2 in his first ten fights—were constant, anticipated and unavoidable. But Backus had to bear in mind that any such juxtaposition with a fighter as great as Basilio is flattery. Even harder to take, let alone believe—especially considering the size of his hometown—were the collations to another Canastota fighter, Dickie DiVeronica. (One wonders if alliteration was a pugilistic prerequisite.) Backus, in his seventh pro fight, fought Marcel Bizien on January 23, 1963, and battled him to a draw. DiVeronica, however, also fought Bizien in 1961 and, later, in 1969 and beat him both times. Backus just couldn't escape the comments, and perhaps he needed to.

After his fourth loss, at the hands of solid Doylestown, Pennsylvania scrapper Billy Anderson, few if any boxers would have gone any further, yet Billy did. A family man—on November 11, 1963, he celebrated his third anniversary with the former Peggy Puglino—Billy was supporting more than himself. The couple's first son, John, was born in 1962. With his time divided between the railroad, construction and working in a (sausage) factory, boxing wouldn't even become a full-time avocation until 1967.

Enter "Mantequilla"

Jose Angel Napoles, alias "Mantequilla" for his smooth-as-butter ring maneuvers, is ranked by most boxing historians in their "Top Fifty Boxers of All Time." He was a ring technician, delivering fierce combinations in perfect synchronization. Smooth and comfortable in the ring, he churned his opponents like cream— almost into a hypnotic state—before spreading them across the canvas.

Napoles came out of the slums of Santiago de Cuba. As a kid, working his way up through the Havana gyms, he mimicked the moves of the great ones, like Kid Gavilan. With over one hundred amateur bouts under his belt, he turned pro on August 2, 1958. Throwing his very first punch—a prelude to prominence— he knocked out his opponent in his professional debut.

After Cuban president Fidel Castro banned pro boxing in 1961, Napoles defected to Mexico, where he was warmly greeted by other famous fighters and adopted as a national hero. He took on "all comers" in his new home and quickly forged a reputation as a fierce ring warrior. At the end of 1963, he was ranked an impressive, if not intimidating, 27-4-0.

1964

This year began with so much promise—four straight wins (three by KO) over: undefeated Canadian welterweight Colin Fraser, a very capable Dave Hilton, a streaky Lou Anderson and a rematch with Colin Fraser—but seemed to disintegrate for Backus under two consecutive point losses: Genaro Soto and Billy Anderson in a rematch. It is these inconsistent times, often at the beginning or end of a fighter's career, that can really challenge the mind. They can undermine one's confidence, even plant an element of doubt. It would soon become clear that they had taken their toll on Backus. On a positive note, two of his opponents would go on to battle future hall of fame members. Dave Hilton would box Luis Manuel Rodriguez (1971), and Genaro Soto would box Ismael Laguna (1969).

Jose Napoles took five fights during the year—one in Japan, one in Venezuela and three in Mexico—and won all five by knockout. Perhaps even more impressive, he needed only seventeen rounds to accomplish the task. Napoles was on his fight game. He was a recognized Mexican star, optimistic about his promise and confident that stateside promoters would take notice.

1965

Billy Backus wasn't scheduled to fight until spring—a reprieve perhaps. Mckeesport light welterweight Rudy Richardson had him slated for March in Johnstown, Pennsylvania. The uninspiring Richardson, having lost four of his last five fights, had little expectations other than a paycheck. In his last fight, a loss against an impressive Doug Agin, he had, however, managed to go the six-round distance. After eight rounds with Backus, Richardson would go the distance again, this time to an unexpected win. The devastating loss, on his twenty-second birthday, plunged Billy Backus into depression and an early retirement.

Napoles took five fights—four in Mexico and one in Venezuela. He knocked out four out of five opponents to notch a quintet of victories. Only Chicago's Eddie Perkins, who was trying desperately to stay in the welter title picture, was able to go the distance. Perkins had both the WBC and WBA light welterweight titles, having defeated Bunny Grant, but he lost them both in a tough split-decision battle to Carlos Hernandez in January.

1966

Boxing is intensely personal. With minimal protection and extensive exposure, little separates the soul from adversity. It is not for the faint at heart or the weak-minded. Distress as a result of personal humiliation must be constantly weighed against reward, for in no other short-term physical activity can a monetary value be so quickly assessed and put upon a participant.

Boxing is not a pastime; the training is painstaking and protracted. The punishment a fighter must endure, even to become a worthy challenger, is inconceivable to most. Indefatigability, as noted author Joyce Carol Oates may refer to it, must be driven by pure instinct.

Boxing is controlled by skill. It is not determined by possession but by ring artistry. Concentration is paramount. It has to be—the possibility of death lingers, albeit improbable. A split-second distraction can be disastrous. Nobody is playing; it is not a game.

Boxing is a timed spectacle without words, only resonance. A spectator can close his eyes and tell by the distinct sound who is winning and who is not. It can be eerie, but it can also be seductive. An enemy can be external—animate, such as an opponent, or inanimate, such as a clock. It can also be internal, psychological. While one considers that boxing can

The boxing license of Canastota's Billy Backus.

be a metaphor for life—and many have, including writers—not all find it such a winsome comparison.

Billy Backus was a husband and a father, a neighbor and a friend. But was Billy Backus a boxer? He had to ponder all of these roles in 1966, a year in which he remained inactive inside the ring. The term "boxer" has its connotations.

Six fights, all in Mexico, yielded Napoles five wins and a rare loss. He knocked out two American fighters to begin the year—Hawaiian Johnny Santos (KO3) and Californian Al Grant (TKO4)—before knocking out Panamanian Humberto Trottman (KO2). In August, he took a fight with Youngstown, Ohio boxer Langston Carl (L.C.) Morgan. Fighting out of Mexico for months, Morgan entered the bout having been a previous Napoles knockout victim (1965-KO3). He was far from optimistic about his next encounter with the fighter. If Napoles was vulnerable to anything, he thought, it was cuts, and they were his downfall on this day during a fourth-round loss. The fighter would rebound quickly, however, and TKO his next two opponents to complete his year.

1967

It was Clarence Darrow who said, "It is not the strongest of the species that survive, nor the most intelligent, but the one most responsive to change." Backus was no Clarence Darrow, nor a barrister, but he could heed good advice and did—the first sign of champion.

The fall of 1967 was turbulent, not only in America but also worldwide. While it was a tempestuous time, it was also an introspective one, especially for the youth in America. Weighing all of his options, Billy Backus decided to look back into the ring. Perhaps it was due to a gym visit with his Uncle Joey, Carmen's brother, that convinced him; or Tony Graziano pushing Billy to take some fights he had booked in Worcester; or simply being laid off from work. Whatever the case, Backus was off to Massachusetts. For two successive Mondays in October, he shook off a little ring rust with a knockout on each. The victories, only a week apart, were uplifting. A six-round TKO over Curtis Phillips—the third Backus opponent to fight a future hall of fame member, Marvin Hagler—at the Syracuse War Memorial Auditorium added more confidence. The initial results of the ring volte-face were promising.

On November 30, it was off to a cold Portland, Maine, to face Gene Herrick. Backus, in his last fight of the year and only three fights out of retirement, was facing the most experienced fighter of his life. On paper it looked like a death wish, as Herrick was a New England middleweight champion with more than twice as many wins than losses and over fifty fights under his belt. But the ten-round Thursday night fight lasted only six as Backus took the TKO victory. For Backus, now fully committed to boxing, his strategy of reclamation had commenced.

"He had drifted away from the sport," recalls manager Graziano. "He had a lot to think about. Life outside the ring wasn't that good. He'd stop by the gym once in awhile, and I knew it was just a matter of time." But any layoff for a fighter can prove difficult, as recovering one's athletic prowess requires a recommitment to training, even a psychological reassessment.

For Napoles, despite four knockouts during only sixteen rounds of Mexican boxing, it was an unimpressive year. Not taking a fight until June—nearly six months off—the most difficult ring challenge Napoles faced was Kansas fighter Johnny Brooks. Slipping of late, Brooks could churn only seven rounds before the osculation of the canvas. Napoles then kayoed fighter-turned-punching-bag L.C. Morgan (KO2) before finishing the year with two tomato cans.

1968

Backus began 1968 with two distance decisions over prosaic opponents— Juan Ramos and Danny Andrews—both at home in the War Memorial Auditorium in Syracuse. Neither fighter had a winning record, but Ramos did go on to fight hall of fame member Emile Griffith (1971), and Andrews had just come off an impressive second-round kayo of veteran Dave Hilton. It was a good kickoff with no overwhelming obstacles.

In May, again at the War Memorial Auditorium, Backus battled a familiar ring veteran, Dick French. The Providence boxer, with an over sixty-fight provenance, had battled some good fighters, including a young Billy Backus back in 1963. But a different Canastota southpaw dropped French three times on the way to a sixth-round TKO.

Three fights and three wins into the year, Backus was scheduled for two summer engagements in New Orleans. He had never fought there before. The first was against a soon-to-be-familiar New Orleans boxer named Percy Pugh in June. The two would clash four times in less than thirteen months. Pugh, having fought over forty fights, had some mileage under his belt but had won nine straight crusades, including a ten-round unanimous decision over Joe Brown. He was also the number two–rated welterweight. Backus mounted an otiose offensive that yielded Pugh the ten-round victory. The duel so impressed "Crescent City" promoter Lou Messina and his principal rival, Jimmy White, that Backus was invited back. He then battled hometown welter Jerry Pellegrini in July. Pellegrini, who had also lost to Pugh three bouts ago, had defeated Joey Durelle and even Canastota's Dickie DiVeronica. Although he would go the distance against Backus, whom he would fight three times, he lost the controversial split decision.

Backus then returned to Syracuse long enough to TKO former opponent Curtis Phillips in a September rematch before leaving once again for the "Big Easy." Inside the Municipal Auditorium in October, he tackled Wichita veteran Johnny Brooks. Although he had lost nine of his last eleven fights, Brooks had brawled with some outstanding boxers in his career, including Jose Napoles the previous year and Emile Griffith (1966). In a good crusade, Backus took the ten-round concordant verdict. A pair of TKOs back at home concluded the year for Billy: the first over Vince Shomo in his last professional fight and the second over Brooklyn bull's-eye Freddie Cobb.

Recap

At 8-1 for the year, a confident and sharper Billy Backus was unmistakable. The trip to New Orleans was ring politics but a nice change for the fighter, who took only one loss. Easing into his competition—a third of his opponents had losing records—it was time to look onward in talent, a point Graziano understood and would corroborate in 1969. Considering it was the fighter's first full year back in the ring, the Backus camp had managed to position and burnish its boxer for the upcoming year. A metamorphosis had taken place, with a new fighter emerging.

"Mantequilla" disposed of seven fighters, all but two with winning records, five via kayo and two via points. Most impressive were his victories—first-round spectacles—over Philly fighter Leroy Roberts (TKO1) and Guyana's Lennox Beckles (KO1). For Napoles, now sharper than the finest imported cheese, it was just a matter of the right opportunity. One of the opponents he disposed of was Herbie Lee, just over a year removed from beginning his fight trilogy with Canastota's own Dickie DiVeronica. As the year closed, Napoles had now fought well over fifty ring battles with only four losses.

1969

Billy Backus would fight seven times during the year against only four different opponents, two of whom he had already faced. He would clash with Percy Pugh three times, winning twice in Syracuse but losing in New Orleans. Between the two Syracuse Pugh fights, he TKO'd Jersey fighter C.L. Lewis, who might as well have been the writer C.S. Lewis, at the War Memorial Auditorium. He then combated Jerry Pellegrini in a pair of back-to-back harmonious decisions. The first fight, held in New Orleans, went to hometown boy Pellegrini, followed by the next, held in Syracuse, which—you guessed it—went to Backus. Hey, it's boxing!

In the final fight of the year, on Halloween night, Backus took on veteran welter Ricky Ortiz at the War Memorial Auditorium in Syracuse. Although the Bronx fighter was coming off a win against Curtis Phillips, he had lost ten of his last fourteen fights. Ortiz, who began his career in 1960, was a city fighter with dreams. Like many, his career began first fighting out of St. Nicholas Arena and working his way up through the local competition, hopefully on to a Garden card. A slipping career means the competition no longer comes to you, and that is how Ortiz ended up in Syracuse. The lackluster battle ended in a disappointing draw.

Recap

Improved competition, with better results, saw a contending Backus finish the year at 4-2-1. He was in the welter mix because he had done what his team has asked him to do—win. But the pieces must fall before they can fit into the title picture. That would take a bit of luck, and Graziano knew it. "Grazi[ano] you worry to much!" became a popular Backus promulgation. "Our Billy," as he was slowly becoming known around town, was confident, but not cocky, and clearly in greater control. He had faith in his team and enjoyed the possessive adjective the town had placed before his name.

Meanwhile, Jose Napoles had become a victim of ring politics. It took hall of fame promoter George Parnassus to come out of retirement to "right the wrongs" that he saw in the Napoles debacle—no solid fighter would enter Mexico to meet him, and no promoter in the United States would import ranking Mexican fighters. On April 18, 1969, all of that changed when "Mantequilla" took on Curtis Cokes for both the WBA/WBC world welterweight titles. The Forum in Inglewood, California, was the site, and a little butter and a barrage of fierce combinations were all that was needed to slide the veteran champion Cokes out of the title chair. By the end of the thirteenth, Cokes could no longer answer; his right eye was closed, and blood streamed over his cheek and onto what remained of his lower lip.

Napoles then successfully defended his belt in a rematch against Cokes and in an undivided decision over Emile Griffith. Like Cokes, Griffith was a gifted fighter; both boxers, along with Napoles, are members of the International Boxing Hall of Fame.

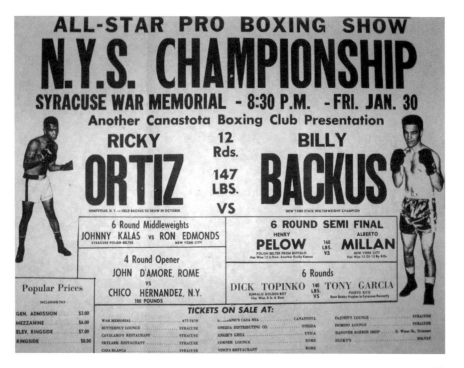

A boxing poster for the Backus rematch with Ricky Ortiz, Friday, January 30, 1970. *Courtesy IBHOF.*

1970

The 1960s ended, and the first year of the next decade would be one that Billy Backus would never forget. The fighter had a few months to ponder the Ortiz draw and confront some tough criticism regarding his performance. To contend, he must not only perform but also excel, for then and only then would he remain in the title mix. It would all begin with a rematch against Ortiz.

Back inside the War Memorial Auditorium on January 30, both fighters entered the ring at exactly 147 pounds. They were greeted this time by referee Jack Milicich rather than Tony Phillips. The other two judges were the same: Tony DeSalvo and Joe Palmer. Right from the start the fight had a different feel to it, be it the contrasting winter chill versus a warm autumn day or simply a brand-new decade. Backus fought noticeably more determined with crisper punches. An insipid Ortiz suffered a bruised right hand and couldn't fight beyond the eighth round. The fight was ruled a TKO victory for Backus. For Ortiz, it was the beginning of the end; he lost eight of his next ten altercations. Upstate fight fans would witness his final professional fight at the arena in Binghamton on October 23, 1975, against Vito Antuofermo.

On March 24, Manuel Burgo was slated for the auditorium to scrap with Backus. Burgo had been plagued by problems, having fought only once in 1969 and not at all in 1968; he even lost a title. In August 1967, he met Dick French for the New England welterweight title in New Bedford. While Burgo won the fight, and the title, on points, he was later stripped of the designation when it was learned that he was over the thirty-five-year age limit. He wouldn't fare much better in Syracuse, as Backus won a unanimous decision.

In the first struggle of the summer, on June 15, Backus faced Flint, Michigan's Frank Steele in Syracuse. With flair to fight the competition, Steele had lost seven of his last ten fights. Nobody at the War Memorial Auditorium felt it would be a quick scuffle though, and it wasn't. The distance decision favored Backus.

The biography of a pugilist is framed by his opponents and enhanced or diminished by his performance against them. Backus's handlers realized that their fighter needed skilled competition to improve, and that's precisely what he faced on July 22, when he met Texas welter Manuel Gonzalez. The veteran fighter had lost only one of his last ten fights. Having fought Curtis Cokes, Kenny Lane, Joe Brown and Emile Griffith, Gonzalez was a proficient and steady fighter with a firm knockout punch. He, like other welter contenders, was trying to situate himself for another title bout. He lost to Emile Griffith in a 1965 WBA/WBC title bout and to Curtis Cokes in a 1966 WBA world welterweight title bout. Not one to venture far from the "Lonestar State," Gonzalez visited Central New York for the first, and last, time of his career.

From the opening bell, Backus would besiege his opponent with a vicious body attack. The assault finally concluded when the tough Texan conceded to the onslaught and dropped to the canvas in the second round. Gonzalez then regained his composure, settled into a pace and began taking middle rounds, but it proved too little too late, and the decision went to Backus. The loss sent Gonzalez into a skid; he would lose sixteen of his next twenty professional fights. Two fights after Backus, he was knocked out at the 1:40 mark of the sixth round in a battle with the best in his class, Jose Napoles.

On October 3, a sharp Billy Backus would engage Detroit's Denny Stiletto. While the Motor City welter had won five of his last ten fights, he was coming off a devastating first-round knockout by a very powerful Rodrigo Valdez back on December 12 (1969). Having not fought since,

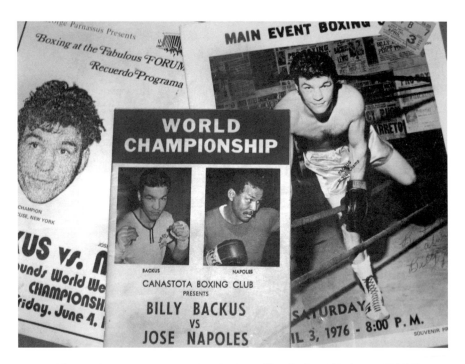

Assorted Backus fight programs, including Backus v. Napoles I and II. *Courtesy IBHOF.*

the fighter-turned-kamikaze decided to enter the ring with Backus. The Detroit boxer, who may have well been standing in a pair of stilettos, hit the canvas in the eighth round. Naturally, the crowd inside the War Memorial Auditorium was thrilled by the performance. Five fights this year and five wins. "Our Billy" needed only one more victory for a perfect 6-0! But that opponent, or mountain to climb, couldn't get much higher or better than Jose Angel Napoles.

The Fight

Napoles opened the year with a successful TKO title defense over Ernie Lopez followed by a third-round knockout over Edwin Mack. On October 5, 1970—the fight before Billy Backus—he would also successfully dispose of Pete Toro at Madison Square Garden; Toro would be dropped twice before the bout was stopped in the ninth. Champions have options, far more than challengers, and Billy Backus was a December (3) alternative.

Over a decade removed from Basilio's duels against DeMarco or his slugfests against Saxton, the city of Syracuse was renewed with fistic pride as it hosted a very special Thursday evening of boxing. The Canastota Boxing Club was pleased to present a world welterweight championship fight, scheduled for fifteen rounds. Anticipation permeated the walls of the War Memorial Auditorium as alliterative echoes—Backus…Basilio…Billy—filled the tiled hallways and staircases. "Our Billy" was the underdog and was still relatively unknown beyond Central New York. The champion's reputation preceded him, but not by much, as this was only his eighth fight in the United States. Napoles, stoic and nonchalant, considered the fight nothing more than a tuneup for his next significant title defense, against Hedgmon Lewis.

Naturally, politics play an enormous role in any title fight, as do logistics. Contract negotiations can be long and very specific, with everybody and everything accounted for. The entire Backus team, led by Graziano, conducted itself masterfully during the process. From the glory-filled promise of the amateur days until the Johnstown disaster (Richardson loss), Graziano had served as Backus's sole—or, more appropriately, soul—manager. Fight matchmaking being what it was, there was no way Napoles manager Cuco Conde would allow his fighter to venture into foreign territory—Syracuse—and put the title on the line without a return fight clause in the contract. Such was indeed the case, so Napoles was guaranteed a fallback should the impossible happen. The fight would also have been implausible had the Napoles camp not trusted the Backus bunch, a point that would be secured by Graziano's relationship with promoter George Parnassus.

The trainer for Jose Napoles was Angelo Dundee, no stranger to the fight game or the Basilio bloodline. But with his fighter, Muhammad Ali, battling Oscar Bonavena on November 7, he was finding it difficult to manage the logistics required for him to work in Napoles's corner in Syracuse. Conde hadn't formally requested Dundee's services, and although the two had an understanding, Dundee wasn't going to press his attendance. So there would be no Dundee magic bag in Napoles's corner. Execution can have a dual meaning during a title contest.

On the day Ronald Reagan was reelected governor of California and Jimmy Carter was elected governor of Georgia, Billy Backus threw his hat into a different ring, looking for an upset of his own. An exuberant, albeit partisan, auditorium crowd of fewer than eight thousand cheered its fighter's introduction; others also watch via closed-circuit television in Mexico and several U.S. cities.

First-round action saw both fighters, centered in the ring, conducting a cautious counterclockwise assault. Napoles, a trim 144 pounds, was measuring with his left jab and, when he felt confident or locked in, firing a swift right uppercut. But the Napoles punches were failing to connect. Backus, at 145½ pounds and shorter, was trying to keep his right positioned to block a left jab. He was also hoping to use it effectively to deliver a barrage when needed. If he could time Napoles's left jab, Backus could deliver his rights to the face of his opponent, making contact with cut targets. Although both fighters landed a few kidney punches, neither was working the body. Backus was also keeping his left tight to the body to block Napoles's powerful right. As the round ended, there had been no clinches—no fighter against the ropes—and neither fighter was in trouble. Napoles, in control, kept his opponent off balance and in check with his left jab. It appeared to be a routine title defense.

As the second opened, Backus was keeping his left higher, possibly to avoid some head damage, while moving it slightly away from the body. Confident that he had the speed to avoid the right, he could take more chances with his southpaw arsenal. However, Backus couldn't connect with his right, as it missed wildly, landing around Napoles's neck. The champion remained patient, still firing with the left jab, measuring, looking inside for an opportunity with that powerful right. As both fighters continued to go to the head, Backus was scoring with his left. The action had picked up as both warriors exhibited greater movement and speed. Napoles's lightning-fast right continued to miss—thankfully so for Backus. The referee, Jack Milicich, reminded Backus to keep his punches up just before the round ended. Midway through the round, slight cuts were opened over both fighters' right eyes.

In what may arguably have been the best round in Billy Backus's career, both fighters moved center ring, with Napoles firing an opening left jab to his opponent's visage. Backus's left was now even higher to protect his forehead. While this opened up Backus's body, the champion paid no attention, choosing instead to look north. Backus continued to stay out of range of Napoles's powerful right, and this frustrated the Cuban. As Napoles brought his hands down, his face was left open to a snappy right jab from Backus. The fight then moved inside. The crowd ringside could hear shouts—"Move right, move to the right!" and "Stay away from that jab!"—originating in Billy's corner. Following the first clinch and separation of the battle, both fighters then began an onslaught of quick combinations. Backus landed a solid right to the head, countered by a Napoles right. The Canastota fighter managed to open a cut over his opponent's left eye; the glass eyebrows of the champion were now vulnerable. But a hard combination to the jaw stunned Backus. It was followed by a driving "Mantequilla" left that sent the Canastota boxer toward the ropes. It looked as if Napoles was going to try to trap him there. But Backus, in a tremendous defensive move, fired a left that backed up Napoles. Backus then used his head—it would later be claimed that butts were responsible for Napoles's cuts—and upper body to leverage his opponent and back him into the center of the ring. It was an experienced move from Backus, one that may have saved him from tremendous damage. Napoles, now bloodied, returned to his corner.

Going into the fourth round, both judge Joe Palmer and referee Jack Milicich had scored the fight two rounds Napoles and one round even, while judge Tony DiSalvo had it two rounds the champion and one round Backus. Although Napoles's trainer, Alfredo Cruz, managed to stop the bleeding briefly between rounds, he couldn't negate the damage.

Spectators were now at the edge of their seats; those who couldn't see the impairment over Napoles's left eye could certainly sense it by the action. Backus then landed another good right to the brow, engaging the cut and opening another. Napoles again moved his left glove up to his forehead to wipe away the gore. Backus peered into his opponent's face, and then his eye socket, watching the blood flow out of the leather-induced incisions. One minute into the round, the referee wisely called in the ringside physician.

A statue, sculpted by Earl Durand, of "Our Billy" greets fight fans entering the International Boxing Hall of Fame.

One look at the wounds, and damage, yielded a recommended stoppage. The referee then "waved it off." Napoles had lost.

For many, Backus was the classic ring contender on a cold winter weekday, battling an opponent regardless of what belt he was wearing (Billy never cared) to reach that tissue-thin difference between a thing done admirably and a thing done ill—an Updikian observation. If boxing careers are judged in terms of proficiency and attainment, his dissertation had been delivered, defended and approved. As he returned to his corner and lifted his gloves in victory, manager Tony Graziano grabbed him from behind and lifted him up. On this night, "Our Billy" had done well and wore the belt of a titleholder, a new world welterweight champion.

UPSTATE NEW YORK

Most Controversial Ring Battles II

Syracuse	March 25, 1949	Nick Barone v. Joe Taylor	W10	State Fair decision causes Chaos!
Syracuse	August 4, 1949	Johnny Taylor v. Jesse Jenkins	D4	MacArthur Stadium crowd confused; both fighters cut!
Syracuse	March 29, 1950	Nick Barone v. Reuben Jones	L10	Fans attack the referee at the State Fair Coliseum!
Syracuse	September 18, 1953	Kid Gavilan v. Carmen Basilio	W15	"Ya godda be kidding!
Syracuse	July 17, 1959	Dick Tiger v. Rory Calhoun	L10	Infuriated War Memorial fans toss trash!
Buffalo	February 12, 1968	Vic Brown v. Johnny Barrazza	TKO2	Barrazza explodes after fight stopped, then attacks Brown!

Selected entries

6

The International Boxing
Hall of Fame

It appeared inside Canastota's *Bee-Journal* in August 1982—an unvarnished article, premeditated yet unfeigned, that would change how the town would be viewed forever. The write-up explained that a quarter of a century had passed since Carmen Basilio had undertaken "serious preparation" (as if an opponent would even consider an alternative) for his first fight against Sugar Ray Robinson. The conquest: a world middleweight championship. The forum: Yankee Stadium on September 23, 1957. It was so great a ring battle that it was given the distinction "1957 Fight of the Year" by the *Ring* magazine. It was so superb a victory that Canastota residents reapportioned their hearts—another beat goes to Basilio.

A conversation at the American Legion led to local resident Joe Bonaventura and Ferrell Miller writing a letter to the newspaper stating their claim: a delinquency of recognition for Canastota's then-favorite son. The dispatch also stated that anyone interested in solving this issue should attend a public meeting at the Legion. The response was far from overwhelming, but it was still a riposte worthy of acknowledgement. Bonaventura, Charlie Bidinger, Pete Finn, Mike Milmoe, Jack Rogers, Don Shuler and Don VanDuesen all attended that first meeting. As the memories came flooding back, more and more ideas began to surface, from naming a street or a park in Basilio's honor to commissioning a plaque or perhaps even a statue. It was also becoming increasingly clear that Joe Bonaventura's point had been well taken—the community needed to honor its hero.

In 1989, numerous former champions witnessed the ribbon-cutting ceremony and opening of the dynamic International Boxing Hall of Fame.

A second meeting brought further information regarding statue costs and even estimates for a building. As donations were being made and the hat passed, everyone remained optimistic. But the $15 collected for the newly formed treasury was far from the $30,000 figure that most felt was needed. It was clear that the labor of love was going to be an arduous task. But spirits were not diminished, as the group anticipated considerable construction assistance and even material donations.

By December 1982, the word had spread, igniting even more interest. Since inquisitiveness spawns ideas, not to mention interrogation, it wasn't long before the question was posed: "Doesn't Canastota have two world champions?" Indeed, the Carmen Basilio Memorial Committee quickly became the group in charge of creating a Basilio-Backus boxing showcase.

The first down payment for a statue, to be created by sculptor Earl Durand of Cinnatus, was put up by a combination of seven men, each offering $250. Artist in residence for many years for the New York State Parks Department, Durand would prove the perfect choice. Using old photographs of Basilio, he created likenesses in clay that not only ignited interest within the Canastota group but also brought the artist closer to his subject. The craftsman's excitement for the project even inspired him to produce a detailed sketch of what would prove to be the building dedicated in 1984.

In addition to restoration at Boldt Castle on the St. Lawrence River and at the historic village of New Harmony, Indiana, Durand's work has been featured on a carving for the Stickley Furniture Company and even on a medal for the Hamilton Mint, part of its Sculptor's America series. In retrospect, his involvement in the showcase couldn't have been a finer choice.

As decisions were made, responsibilities increased, necessitating a greater meeting frequency. In another sign of community commitment, Rusty Woolsey donated weekly meeting space at the Rusty Rail. Tasks such as fundraising also required organization; the Boxing Hall of Fame Incorporated was formed in 1982. Serving as officers were Joseph A. Bonaventura, president; Charlie J. Sgroi, vice-president; Edward P. Brophy, treasurer; and Charles C. Bidinger, secretary. Progress was being made. Spirits, occasionally fragile, were often uplifted by large donations that sustained momentum—a critical factor for success and proof, in the eyes of many, that the project was indeed viable.

In March 1983, the fundraising efforts were officially launched with a dinner to be held at the White Elephant. The event attracted fans from all over Upstate New York, as an overflow crowd saluted both Carmen and Billy. A profit of $2,000 was realized from the event, thanks to a $1,000 gift from the Genesee Brewing Company and a herculean effort by Paul Basilio, who donated the evening's culinary delights. You guessed it, Basilio sausage!

T-shirts proclaiming the mission, now a collector's item, became the most popular fundraising method. "It seemed we hawked shirts everywhere," said Chuck Sgroi. "We sold them at fight film nights and area promotions." Even an escape weekend raffle was held in order to bring the committee closer to its goal.

As the showcase became more of a physical existence, some contention arose regarding a site. The McDonald's location at the thruway, always a majority choice, was selected over a place downtown or in Clark Park. The generous donation of land by restaurant owner David Beach finally made it an actuality. Building began once the arduous task of deed transferal was complete.

Many people assisted in the venture: Bob Arnold, video advice; Gary Bruno, land transfer; Harry Hood, tax work; and Mike Perretta, incorporation and bylaws. Relentless workers during the entire process included John E. Emmi (trustee), Joe Eppolito, Fred Eppolito, Felix Montalbano, Joseph A. Paone (trustee), Joe Rinaldo, Richard Rinaldo, Jack W. Rogers (trustee) and Ada Sgroi.

Rocco Altamuro, deemed "clerk of the works," became a guiding force behind the showcase, soliciting labor and much-needed material. Craftsman contributing their efforts included Bill Ackeran, Otto Altamuro, Mike Armstrong, Aaron Dewey, Larry DiGeorge, Sam DiGeorge, Fred Eppolito Sr., Fred Eppolito Jr., Bob Fusillo, George Gleeson, Lyle Hicks, Joe Magliocca, Lyle Materne, Scott Pickard, Frank Pilato, Joe Tomarchio, Mart Tomarchio, Chuck Walsh, Jack White and Jerry White. Material goods contributors included Altamuro Construction, Bonnie Electric, Canastota Constructors, Cataldo Brothers of Rome, DiVeronica Brothers, Galavotti Painting Company, Morrow Grago, John Kime True Value, Madison Glass, Mazzullo & Son, MidState Redi Mix of Oneida and Patane Christopher Gardens. Estimates of the worth of goods and services received topped the $10,000 range. Such generosity is indicative of how a community can join hands for a common goal.

The driving force from the beginning of the process was Edward P. Brophy. He not only accepted his role, but he also embraced it. "Working

The townspeople raised funds for a boxing showcase that would celebrate the achievements of their two local heroes.

full-time on ideas, and fundraising, Eddie seemed perfect from the start," comments Chuck Sgroi.

The boxing showcase was dedicated on August 18, 1984.

THE BIRTH OF THE INTERNATIONAL BOXING HALL OF FAME

Having community support for a project is one thing, but having an entire sport, particularly one as established as boxing, embrace an idea such as an International Boxing Hall of Fame in such a small Upstate New York hamlet seemed a bit far-fetched. Besides, the idea wasn't new, even if the site was.

Unlike Major League Baseball or the National Football League, boxing has no single legislative body, no lone voice for a papal blessing: "This is the one and only boxing hall of fame." There were others already claiming such designation, the most significant being Nat Fleischer's, of the *Ring* (magazine) fame, which was located at the *Ring* headquarters at 120 West Thirty-first Street in New York City and instituted by the publication in 1954. Three groups were elected to this Boxing Hall of Fame: the pioneer group, made up of men who were active in the bare-knuckle days and who did much to establish the sport; the old-timers, made up of fighters active before 1919; and the modern group, boxers who fought after 1919 and had been retired for at least two years. But since Fleischer's death in 1972, the concept had deteriorated. Perhaps there really was an opportunity.

The Boxing Hall of Fame Incorporated, then the driving force in the design and construction of the boxing showcase, began implementing ideas even before its initial mission was met. In fact, once it became clear that the showcase would come to fruition, the momentum shifted toward a larger concept.

By 1984, the political support was in place. Congressman George C. Wortley was excited, as was Senator Alfonso D'Amato, also willing to assist. Governor Mario M. Cuomo had met and even discussed the project personally. Senator Daniel Patrick Moynihan gave it his full support, stating, "Titletown is the ideal site for such a facility." Boxing support was also taking hold. The WBA thought it was "a great idea," and WBC president Jose Sulaiman Chagnon proclaimed, "History should have a place for the boxing people that have written their names as heroes of our sport, and a Hall of Fame ensures that is accomplished." Even as far away as Cape Town, South Africa, approval rang out for the Canastota enterprise.

Following the dedication of the boxing showcase came the backing and financial support for an independent market study conducted by Knowledge Systems & Research, Inc., of Syracuse, New York. This general feasibility study was conducted in close cooperation with Schleicher-Soper, Inc., and the Regional Planning and Development Board. This $35,000 effort reinforced, in the committee's own words, "the CAN in CANASTOTA" and was the result of two state legislative grants and generous donations from local citizenry.

The study concluded that the facility would rely heavily on secondary markets for attendance, emphasis should be on a museum concept/approach rather than on a hall of fame, marketing and fundraising were crucial to the success of the project and operating expenditures must be kept in line with revenue projections.

The Regional Planning and Development Board presented the results of its location analysis on February 19, 1985. Seventeen potential sites were identified within or adjacent to the village of Canastota. They were then divided into three distinct geographic groups: sites around Thruway Exit 34, sites along Route 5 and sites in or near the central business district. The committee then decided to locate the facility in the vicinity of the thruway exit, which meant five potential sites: Thruway North, Thruway South, McDonalds West, Toll Booth Farm or Thruway Triangle. The latter was the final selection.

The Thruway Triangle—a triangular site of about thirteen acres—is bounded by the eastbound lane of the thruway, with an exit ramp, and by North Peterboro Street to the west. Similar to other sites, the logistics, such as soil, drainage, utilities and even zoning, made sense. The potential site development costs were estimated at about $220,000, which included the acquisition and demolition of a single-family home. This was on a separate parcel on the southwest corner of the site, owned by Kathy Eddy. Upon the successful acquisition of the proposed site, demolition commenced.

"I kept driving by and watching them, including Eddie [Brophy], tearing down the walls, and when they were finished, all that was basically left was the foundation," recalled Chuck Sgroi. It was that substructure that would eventually yield the museum in its opening phase, which took place on June 8, 1989. The two-thousand-square-foot museum was the initial step necessary to plant the seed firmly at 1 Hall of Fame Drive. The building's design, executed by Wentworth Construction, was conducive to both required exhibit space and future expansion—a perfect fit! As the displays were added and enhanced in January 1990, preparation was underway for the museum's first class of inductees.

The International Boxing Hall of Fame

It surprises some to learn that the initial design and construction of the proposed museum was very aggressive. A proposed two-story main hall, encompassing 30,368 square feet, including a 220-seat auditorium, was envisioned as a focal point on the proposed site. It was to be a phased construction beginning with this main hall, followed by Phase II (a second facility housing exhibit space and conference facilities) and then Phase III (a third building that included a multiuse arena). The entire concept was to be sold to sponsors through the use of an elaborate die-cut color brochure complete with four multipage inserts. "The Pursuit of Excellence" became the initial mission but, in retrospect, was far too aggressive for both sponsors and the community.

THE MUSEUM'S FIRST EXPANSION

The success of the institution led to an increase in donations in the form of boxing artifacts and funding. This combination made expansion not only necessary but also achievable. On August 15, 1992, a new five-hundred-square-foot east wing was added to the existing structure. The additional space allowed for new exhibits and also included a much-needed business office. This also meant that the downstairs of the facility, which had once housed the exhibits, could be modified into a research center. Additional exhibits, with larger pieces, could now be accommodated, as could the administration of a more efficient business office, all through the generosity of the WBC ($10,000) and Shelly Finkel ($2,500).

THE INTERNATIONAL BOXING HALL OF FAME EVENT PAVILION

The pavilion grew out of numerous proposals that had been floating around for years. The concept used the undeveloped land around the site to become a more visible attraction. The goal was to have the traffic along the New York State Thruway, from both directions, see and recognize the museum well in advance of the exit. The expansion would also provide additional parking space and workable sites to accommodate the increased attendance during Induction Weekend.

The Lewiston Construction Corporation of Fayetteville, New York (Syracuse suburb), undertook the ten-thousand-square-foot task. The

Thousands of boxing fans from around the world assemble annually at the hall of fame's events pavilion during Induction Weekend.

facility, which opened in the spring of 2003, includes a business office, a set of restrooms, an expansive display area and a large storage space. Outside, it provides a staging area complete with a flexible amphitheatre capable of seating about seven hundred during Induction Day ceremonies.

THE MADISON SQUARE GARDEN RING

"After 82 years of use, the world-famous boxing ring from Madison Square Garden—which was retired in September 2007—was being shipped 270 miles north to Canastota, New York," read an announcement. On January 12, 2008, the historic surround was assembled, for one last time, and put on permanent display inside the event pavilion at the International Boxing Hall of Fame.

The ring made its debut on December 11, 1925, when Paul Berlenbach and Jack Delaney fought for the light heavyweight title, and it was last used on June 10, 2007, when Miguel Cotto and Zab Judah met for the welterweight

After eighty-two years of use, the world-famous boxing ring from Madison Square Garden has found a permanent home.

title. A list of "the Garden" ring fighters reads like a who's who of boxers, including Muhammad Ali, Henry Armstrong, Tony Canzoneri, Roberto Duran, Arturo Gatti, Kid Gavilan, Rocky Graziano, Evander Holyfield, Pernell Whitaker, Joe Louis, Rocky Marciano, Mike Tyson, Ezzard Charles, Oscar De La Hoya, George Foreman, Sugar Ray Robinson, Carmen Basilio, Alexis Arguello and many, many more.

"This is by far the most famous ring in the sport of boxing. Madison Square Garden is the 'Mecca of Boxing' and the ring at 'the Garden' that so many gladiators fought in is truly one of the most significant artifacts in sports history," said International Boxing Hall of Fame executive director Edward Brophy.

The boxing ring was also used for title fights, at Yankee Stadium and the Polo Grounds, and even for promotional stunts, such as exhibition bouts in Times Square, on 125th Street and in front of the Nathan's hot dog stand in Coney Island.

Operation

The June Induction Weekend, as expected, takes center stage, as annual planning is extensive and labor intensive. No sooner are the tents on the grounds disassembled than planning begins for the subsequent year. In addition to the day-to-day operations, the year is typically complemented by a handful of events. An annual November fundraiser—often a banquet—is followed by a late December or early January announcement of the year's inductees. A visit from a champion or two, the preview of a film or a book signing is always a possibility, but by spring, everyone's attention is focused on the weekend.

The Future

On the morning of Friday, October 16, 2009, I walked the museum grounds with Executive Director Brophy. Explaining much about what the first twenty years has meant to the institution, the community and the sport it serves, he was reflective but not sentimental. He noted the possibility of a new freestanding research center, aimed at improving education and meeting the expanded research needs of those they serve. When Brophy spoke, it was with no less passion than I had personally witnessed two decades ago—his commitment steadfast, his resolve relentless. He is now surrounded by a small staff of talented individuals and experienced volunteers, and the pieces continue to fall in place.

7

A Gallery of Champions

Nicaragua's Alexis Arguello, a 1992 IBHOF inductee, was a three-division champion and a popular visitor to Canastota.

Virgin Islands boxer Livingstone Bramble is perhaps best remembered by Upstate fans for his 1984 battle with Ray Mancini.

Eddie Futch, a 1994 **IBHOF** inductee, was a gifted trainer and one of the sport's true gentlemen.

Above: Japan's Masahiko "Fighting" Harada, a 1995 IBHOF inductee, was a flyweight and bantamweight world champion. *Courtesy IBHOF.*

Right: Puerto Rican prodigy Wilfred Benitez, a 1996 IBHOF inductee, was a stylish boxer with a powerful punch. *Courtesy IBHOF.*

Left: Héctor Camacho, nicknamed "Macho Camacho," is a colorful and talented Puerto Rican boxer. *Courtesy IBHOF.*

Below: Brooklyn's Carmine Tilelli, a 1993 IBHOF inductee, was better known as Joey Giardello.

Right: Virgin Islands boxer Emile Griffith, a 1990 IBHOF inductee, began boxing under IBHOF trainer Gil Clancy. *Courtesy IBHOF.*

Below: Matthew Saad Muhammad, a 1998 IBHOF inductee, is commonly remembered for his outstanding 1979 title fight against Marvin Johnson.

Ken Norton, a 1992 **IBHOF** inductee, is often recalled for his trilogy with three-time world heavyweight champion Muhammad Ali.

Mexican Rubén Olivares, a 1991 **IBHOF** inductee, is a bantamweight legend and a popular figure in Canastota, New York.

A 1990 IBHOF inductee, Sandy Saddler, a Willie Pep rival, is considered one of the greatest punchers of all time.

Billy Soose, a 2009 IBHOF inductee, caught in a rare visit to Canastota's boxing shrine.

In 1978, in his second year as a professional fighter, Leon Spinks won the heavyweight championship over Muhammad Ali.

Mexican Carlos Zarate, a 1994 IBHOF inductee, was a knockout artist inside the ring.

Muhammad Ali is proof of how the wonderful sport of boxing transcends all borders and inspires our youth. *Courtesy IBHOF.*

UPSTATE NEW YORK

Great Ring Rivalries

Buffalo	1911–1912	Willie Brennan v. Paddy Levin
Buffalo	1913–1918	Jack Britton v. Jimmy Duffy
Buffalo	1914–1924	Johnny Dundee v. Rocky Kansas
Syracuse	1919–1921	Mike O'Dowd v. Young Fisher
Buffalo	1922–1927	Pete Latzo v. Frankie Schoell
Buffalo	1926–1930	Maxie Rosenbloom v. Jimmy Slattery
Buffalo	1932–1933	George Nichols v. Lou Scozza
Buffalo	1937	Ralph DeJohn v. Jimmy Clark
Rochester	1938	Teddy Yarosz v. Ralph DeJohn
Buffalo & Rochester	1941–1947	Joe Muscato v. Johnny Flynn
Rochester & Buffalo	1946	Joey Maxim v. Phil Muscato
Buffalo	1946–1949	Phil Muscato v. Lee Oma
Syracuse & Binghamton	1949-1950	Nick Barone v. Joe Taylor
Syracuse	1949–1950	Nick Barone v. Teddy Yarosz

THE INTERNATIONAL BOXING HALL OF FAME

CNY Boxing Appreciation Award

1987	Norm Rothschild
1988	Roy Simmons Sr.
1989	Irv Robbins
1990	John DeJohn
1991	Al Wertheimer
1992	Pat Nappi
1993	Tony Graziano
1994	Canastota Boxing Club
1995	Dick Tobin
1996	Billy Harris
1997	Don Hamilton
1998	Ray Rinaldi
1999	Tom Coulter
2000	Phil Serling
2001	Greg Sorrentino
2002	Frankie Adams
2003	Dr. Armand Cincotta
2004	Bob Fenocchi
2005	Danny Akers
2006	Peter Cappuccilli, Jr.
2007	Ralph and Rocky Fratto
2008	Paul Barkal

8

A Score to Settle

The Twentieth Anniversary

As the still morning broke on this memorable Sunday, the prelude was simply perfect—fifty-four degrees, on the way to a balmy seventy-four, with moderate humidity. From behind my windshield observation post, I noted some patchy light fog, God's security blanket, lifting off the freshly planted fields along the New York State Thruway. It was difficult not to be a bit sentimental. It was a sojourn made in earnest—a short eighteen-minute journey—to a familiar destination, 1 Hall of Fame Drive, the site of the International Boxing Hall of Fame in Canastota, New York.

Of paramount concern on this day, Induction Day, was the weather; it is, after all, Central New York. Would the forecasted afternoon showers arrive on schedule, or would they delay long enough to keep the ceremonies dry? In Greek mythology, Zeus is the king of the gods, the ruler of Mount Olympus and the god of sky and thunder. Etched in marble, he is the perfect heavyweight. Certainly such a deity wouldn't consider, not even for a moment, altering such perfection. On an afternoon that honors the thunder gods of the ring, as it turned out, he did not.

As I drove through the tollbooth guarding Exit 34 of the primary east–west stretch of the New York State highway system, I was thankful that I could observe and record a town rising to a new dawn on a day that has grown special in the hearts of so many residents. I turned left, away from the museum grounds, heading south on Peterboro Street. A crew of two was installing flags that would line the path of a morning parade route, while a gentleman from the police department carefully placed chairs along a section of the sidewalk—no doubt meant for the town dignitaries who inhabited the offices directly behind. Farther down the street, a young lady,

A quiet Induction Day morning looking north on Peterboro Street in Canastota.

or perhaps entrepreneur may be more appropriate, was moving signs on items set up for a yard sale. Opportunity outside the ring can also be fleeting.

After picking up the Syracuse newspaper, the *Post-Standard*, at a filling station at the corner of Route 5, my voyage south was complete. I then headed north, again along Peterboro Street, retracing my path. The sun, now over my right shoulder, was just rising above the horizon and over the trees in back of the town's Clark Park. The beauty of the moment overtook me, so I stopped for a closer look. Sidestepping the arched iron gates protected by two small cannons on pedestals, I came upon a marble walkway. I followed the simple path to a statue of a soldier in arms. He was attentively facing a wall in recognition of those who served in World War II, individuals who were all too familiar to those who lived here. As I glanced over the names from "Our Greatest Generation," I couldn't help but be humbled and grateful that I had this day because of these brave souls. They fought a different fight for the belt of freedom.

Continuing onward, I parked near the railroad overpass, which now read in large yellow-stenciled font, "Canastota." Thoughts of those who had arrived here by rail years ago were recalled—families in search of a new

The World War II monument at Clark Park.

beginning; immigrants longing for a familiar face. During my reflection, a woman interrupted her morning walk to ask me if I was lost. "Only in the moment," I responded. "Thank you so much for asking."

Ahead, the village had constructed a memorial park. Located in the downtown district next to the post office, the Reflection Park consists of three imperial black, polished granite dies dedicated to the fire department, police department and Greater Lenox Ambulance Service. Each is inscribed with the department's prayer and emblem. A now haunting steel beam from the World Trade Center wreckage is displayed within the park. The park is enclosed with black fencing and surrounded with landscaping. Two fountains have been constructed on each side of the park within the stone block frame. The memorial is dedicated to the members of Canastota's police, fire and ambulance departments who serve their community and to those who lost their lives in the tragic events of September 11, 2001. It was a motionless reminder that much has happened in the course of the last two decades.

Picking up my initial cup of coffee for the day at the Dunkin' Donuts almost directly across the street from the hall of fame, I sat at a table alone

The village of Canastota is located inside the town of Lenox in Madison County, New York.

just to eavesdrop on the morning conversations. Two New York State troopers came in and were chatting about the local activities, as were a group of four gentlemen at the table to my right. "This is incredible," one of the men stated. "My wife lets me come here to relive my dreams."

"This is my weekend," he vehemently adds. "In trade," he continues, "I let her choose a vacation destiny for the both of us, you know Cancun or Jamaica, a place she only dreamed of. I think it's only fair."

Nearby was the boxing showcase; it, too, would be celebrating an anniversary this year—a quarter of a century of existence. This showcase, along with the blood, sweat and tears of the names that adorn its plaque, is the reason why the International Boxing Hall of Fame exists in this small town. It is a monument not only in honor of two great fighters but also of an entire community. Someday a "Founder's Award" should be given out by a committee made up the individuals who were responsible for building this showcase in their honor, not only as a way to recognize an individual for her community service as it relates to the museum but also in hopes that nobody will ever forget these men and women. Frankly speaking, not enough has been done to honor them. Naturally, the years have taken a toll on the structure. Many items are now faded by sunlight. Even the impressive statues of Carmen Basilio and Billy Backus have had to be moved; they are now located inside of the museum across the street. But things essentially remain the same. The triumphs of their gladiators remain intact, and their dream is still alive.

THE VOLUNTEERS

Most of the volunteers began arriving on the museum grounds about 8:30 a.m. Some, including Canastota's Jim Clark, spent hours the night before setting up chairs inside the event pavilion that hosts the formal ceremonies.

"You know whatever you've done, he [Director Edward Brophy] is going to change it!" I shouted over to Clark, approaching him on the museum grounds. A big smile lit up my friend's face. Along with Joe Inman and Gary Phillips, we had been volunteers for years. When I reached him, at the center of the sidewalk, he turned and looked straight into the pavilion. "Oh no," he proclaimed, "we're not centered, the symmetry isn't perfect. [pause] Maybe he won't notice."

Facing the pavilion was a refreshment stand. Inside, T.J. Tornatore was diligently preparing the day's victuals. T.J. had worked repeatedly with Rich Rinaldo and Scott Rapasadi, both veteran volunteers for the museum. When you take a moment to think about it: where else in town can you eat a Basilio sausage, bend the ear of a village trustee (Rapasadi) and enjoy such an array of free activities?

Nanci Knox, DC, spotted me and came over to say hello. Besides being a gifted resident chiropractor, Knox was also a volunteer chairperson, heading up the museum's membership committee. Having not seen me in over two years, she greeted me warmly, as if I never left. That's just like Nanci, always a delight, so indicative of the many who give of their time.

Off in the parking area, I noticed Angelo Testani, another volunteer chairperson, loading up a pushcart with merchandise he took to the dinner in Syracuse the night before. Testani and his brother Anthony, along with Eric Warren, do an outstanding job of handling the gifts and souvenirs for the weekend.

A gentleman in a stylish Yankees hat walked along a walkway connecting the museum grounds to the adjacent parking area (temporary modifications to the museum grounds are common). His glance toward me yielded a point and smile. It was Brett Barnes. He and his wife, Carol, and even his mother-in-law, have become active in the weekend festivities. It's another example of how family plays a role in the weekend. Carol assumed the chairperson role from Betsy Regulbuto, a beloved, longtime and very active volunteer; it was a passing of the torch, so to speak. "We were just talking about you," Brett said as he walked toward me. He then provided me with an overview of the previous night's dinner at the OnCenter in Syracuse.

The familiar face of Doug Gustin, carrying his briefcase, was then spotted. Doug, along with Chuck and Ada Sgroi and a handful of other subjects, would operate one of three tents that line the sidewalk between the museum and the pavilion. Inside the tent, a special United States Postal Service cancellation, especially designed for the event, would be available to visitors on the grounds. The postal tribute—a great touch by the way—was the first event scheduled on Induction Day. "I had the wonderful pleasure of talking to your Mom yesterday," I shouted. His face beamed in a way only a son could reflect. "She enlightened me on your rich family heritage, among other things." Joyce Gustin, Doug's mom, is the perfect example of Canastota charm—a warm, sensitive and caring individual.

A bit later, Doug Gustin spotted the Fullmer contingent from West Jordan, Utah, and called them over to say hello. That's the same Fullmer

Don Fullmer, brother of IBHOF member Gene Fullmer, and Jay Fullmer chats with friends in Canastota.

family that has produced boxers Gene, Don and Jay. Now just think about it for a second. Gene Fullmer, also a member of the hall of fame, was a rival of Canastota's own Carmen Basilio. In the 1959 Fight of the Year, for the vacant National Boxing Association world middleweight title, Fullmer TKO'd Basilio in the fourteenth round. Ten months later, in June 1960, Fullmer took the same decision two rounds sooner. Now, you would think some animosity might still reside with some Basilio fans, but such is not the case in boxing, and such is certainly not the case in Canastota. Quite the contrary, as the Fullmer family—staunch supporters of the hall—are not only welcomed but also cherished by the residents.

As I was listening to Larry, Don's son, talk about his father's exploits at Madison Square Garden and how unfortunate it was that Uncle Gene couldn't make the trip, I noticed Don taking a seat on the nearby bench. At the conclusion of our brief conversation, I went over to sit next to the outstanding middleweight. Don Fullmer fought from 1957 to 1973 and was rated in the top ten of both the middleweight and light heavyweight divisions. He held victories over middleweight champions Emile Griffith and Carl "Bobo" Olson, both in the hall of fame. He defeated WBA world

Ike Williams with Jimmy McLarnin in 1991; the latter began his pro career in 1923. *Courtesy IBHOF.*

heavyweight champion Jimmy Ellis and knocked down world middleweight champion Nino Benvenuti in a losing fifteen-round decision for the world title. Fullmer also battled New York's Joey Archer, Buffalo's Rocky Fumerelle and Levittown's Bobby Cassidy. We chatted uninterrupted for about twenty minutes about everything, from what Canastota means to boxing to fighting Benvenuti not only once, but twice!

The grounds begin filling early with spectators and autograph collectors, identifiable by who was carrying bottled water and a lawn chair versus a backpack and a handful of Sharpies. Many of their faces were recognizable, most having not missed an induction in years. Bo Bilicki was one of those individuals who had not only made it annually to the event but also had migrated from a casual autograph collector and fight lover to a bona fide boxing historian. Hailing from Lockport, Bilicki participated in many elements around the sport, including the Buffalo Veteran Boxers Association–Ring #44. Recognizing Bob Collins, a boxing writer and historian from Rochester, they chatted about their latest boxing treasure hunts or unearthing a long-lost ring battle from yesteryear. That camaraderie and level of dialogue is a large part of what draws Upstate New York fight fans, along with the diverse

Canastota mayor Todd Rouse speaking with Induction Weekend visitor Frank DiPino.

Two Induction Weekend staples, emcee Joey Fiato and hall of fame president Donald Ackerman.

selection of events, aimed at both community interaction and fundraising for the museum.

For example, the day before, at the Casolwood Golf Course, I had run into Tom Shiptenko, a radio station manager for the Equinox Broadcasting Corporation in Johnson City, outside of Binghamton. Shiptenko had been a friend of the museum for decades and an excellent example of how others have carried their mission to every part of the state. As we were talking, I noticed many other familiar faces, even other athletes. Former professional baseball player Frank DiPino from Camillus, outside Syracuse, was there with a friend. DiPino appeared in over five hundred games in twelve seasons with five different ball clubs. "I grew up in the Ali-Frazier era," DiPino expounded, "and followed all the great fighters, especially those with connections to Central New York. I didn't want to miss this."

The festivities on this Induction Day, like those preceding it, began with the arrival of the event emcee, Joey Fiato. His trademark tenor had become a fixture at the event; he was Canastota's Don Dunphy, if you will. Similar to Dunphy, Fiato has introduced some of the greatest names in ring history.

Approaching the event pavilion stage armed with a handful of plaques and rings was hall of fame president Don Ackerman. Sporting a beige suite, white shirt and red tie, Ackerman would oversee inductee introductions. In addition to serving on the board of directors of the museum, he was also a talented ring judge, having scored such bouts as the W. Klitschko v. Ibragimov 2008 title fight at Madison Square Garden; the N'dou v. Malignaggi 2007 IBF light welterweight title fight at Mohegan Sun; and the Houghtaling v. Harris 2003 IBC Americas light welterweight title fight at the Turning Stone Casino in Verona, New York.

Critical to the success of the weekend were other volunteers, not present on the museum grounds this morning. They include Grace Rapasadi, Bob Stokes, Jennifer Warner, Craig Bailey, John Hunt, Alexia Conrad, Jean Palmer, Charlene Lawless, Dr. Juan Kassab, Charlene Barres, Pat Orr, Mike Brophy, Diana Armstrong, Jim Walter, John Beach, Walt Stokes, Randy Smithers, Henry Brown, Carol and Mike Burch, Carol Barnes, Rich Brophy, Ross Stagnitti and Chris Bargabos. Since some events are held offsite, they require a large framework of individuals coordinating every level of detail. Months of planning are required for each event. Many of these individuals, like Grace Rapasadi, have been timeless ambassadors for not only the hall of fame but also the entire town of Canastota. To say that they are all treasures would be an understatement.

Over the years, the stalwart of the institution has been Edward Brophy. But he has been complemented by many, such as Mark and Mary George, Richard Hoppe and Clint Parrott, all contributors to the two decades of existence. The current staff is spearheaded by Jeff Brophy and complemented by the efforts of Chris Bowers, Rachel DiVeronica, Mike Delaney, Dave Wrobel and Cristen Brophy. All have spent countless hours reviewing every aspect of the Induction Weekend.

At a tap on the shoulder, I responded to Pat Prettyman, another veteran volunteer. Prettyman, a talented Syracuse retail manager, her husband, Jimmy, and I share many past memories. It's just amazing how quickly our minds can take us back in time—so many years, so quickly—as if we never left.

The Week's Events

The Twentieth Annual Hall of Fame Induction Weekend had officially begun on Thursday afternoon at 1:00 p.m. and would run until the Farewell Celebration at 3:30 p.m. on this day, Sunday. The schedule, despite some

On-site training is part of the Induction Weekend and may even provide an opportunity to interact with a boxing contender.

modifications, has remained relatively unchanged over the years. There is a comfort level with consistency among the volunteers, staff and attendees.

Three hours' worth of activities had begun the week on Thursday, all conducted on the museum grounds. They featured ringside lectures, celebrity book signings and the official Opening Ceremony. Speaking at the latter event was the first South African boxer to be inducted, Brian Mitchell. "We took an eighteen-hour flight to be here, and it's been worth every minute of it," he said. If that statement doesn't speak for just how important this shrine has become worldwide, nothing does.

Friday began at 10:00 a.m. with ringside lectures, a celebrity workout session and a celebrity fist casting—all held on the museum grounds— followed by "A Night of Rising Stars" dinner at the Rusty Rail Party House in Canastota. The activities then migrated on Saturday to other places around town and into Syracuse. The scheduled events included a golf tournament held at Casolwood Golf Course and a "5K Race, Fun Run" starting at Canastota High School, where a Boxing Autograph Card Show was also held. The museum grounds hosted ringside lectures and a celebrity workout session. Finally, the day's activities were topped

The 2005 film *Cinderella Man* featured two visitors to Canastota, actor Russell Crowe and his trainer, Angelo Dundee. *Courtesy IBHOF.*

off with a VIP Gala cocktail reception held at Greystone (Canastota) and a "Banquet of Champions" held at the Syracuse OnCenter Complex.

The most exciting element for visitors and, in particular, boxing enthusiasts were the guests who showed up at the weekend's events unannounced. The inconspicuous visitors mingled with fans. Over the years, these unexpected guests have included everyone from actors such as Russell Crowe and Daniel Day-Lewis to relatives of inductees and even former sparring partners. I remember seeing the great middleweight Billy Soose casually walking among visitors, almost in shock witnessing the excitement that was taking place around him. Sadly, the fighter would never see his own induction, which occurred two decades after the institution's creation.

With Upstate New York summers being relatively short, it's also common to have coinciding area events. Such had been the case in the past and such was the case again this year, as the Jamesville Balloon Fest(ival) was taking place just outside of Syracuse. The closest event in proximity has always been the Chittenango Oz fest, now renamed Oz-STRAVAGANZA! The L. Frank Baum birthplace and neighboring town holds an annual festival honoring Baum's life and literary works, which include, of course, *The Wonderful Wizard of Oz.*

The Hall of Fame Alumni and Guests

A key element to the success of the weekend has been the attendees, a combination of hall of fame alumni mixed with special guests, current champions, rising stars and selected parade grand marshals. This unique blend, aimed at attracting a diverse group of international visitors, domestic boxing fans and area residents, is a bit of horizontal marketing at its best—and it works!

Hall of fame alumni attending this year included Carmen Basilio, Carlos Ortiz, Emile Griffith, Ruben Olivares, Marvelous Marvin Hagler, Aaron Pryor, Michael Carbajal, Carlos Palomino, Don Chargin, J. Russell Peltz, Stanley Christodoulou, Bert Sugar, Angelo Dundee and Emanuel Steward.

Special guests of the museum in 2009 included Christy Martin, Livingstone Bramble, Marlon Starling, Leon Spinks, Greg Haugen, Mark Breland, Junior Jones, John H. Stracey, Meldrick Taylor, Billy Backus, Dickie DiVeronica, Gaby Canizales, Don Fullmer and Juan LaPorte.

Also a part of this weekend's activities was "A Night of Rising Stars," which highlighted the future of the sport. Those featured at this commemorative dinner included top-ten heavyweight contender Kevin "the Kingpin" Johnson, 2008 Olympic bronze medalist Deontay Wilder, IBF super middleweight champion Lucian Bute, two-time welterweight champion Kermit "the Killer" Cintron, WBC welterweight champion Andre Berto and WBO interim junior middleweight champion Paul "the Punisher" Williams. Hall of fame trainer, manager and HBO world championship boxing expert commentator Emanuel Steward hosted the evening.

This year's hall of fame Parade of Champions grand marshals were legendary actor Burt Young (Paulie from *Rocky*) and *The Sopranos* star Federico Castelluccio. Both spoke fondly of their love for the sport of boxing.

The Inductees

Back on December 9, 2008, the International Boxing Hall of Fame and Museum announced the newest class of inductees to enter the hall. The living inductees included bantamweight champion Orlando Canizales (USA), heavyweight champion Lennox Lewis (UK), junior lightweight champion Brian Mitchell (South Africa), publicist/matchmaker/promoter Bob Goodman (USA), promoter Akihiko Honda (Japan), journalist Hugh McIlvanney (UK) and broadcaster Larry Merchant (USA).

The hall of fame also released names of posthumous honorees: middleweight champion William (Gorilla) Jones, welterweight champion "Mysterious" Billy

The United Kingdom's Lennox Lewis, a 2009 inductee, spends a quiet moment before an Induction Weekend event.

Smith and middleweight champion Billy Soose in the old-timer category; manager Billy Gibson and commissioner Abe J. Greene in the nonparticipant category; journalist Paul Gallico in the observer category; and Tom Hyer in the pioneer category. Inductees were voted on by members of the Boxing Writers Association and a panel of international boxing historians.

Excitement builds, as speculation in town surrounds which of the living inductees will choose to attend the formal ceremony. Twenty years ago, there were simply no guarantees; it wasn't so easy to convince everyone of the museum's legitimacy. But today, one can be almost certain of perfect attendance. Supported by a family of returning inductees, envious guests, a wealth of rising superstars and thousands of visitors, a far different canvas has been painted.

THE INDUCTION

"Our sport is usually looked at as a brutal, savage sport," Lennox Lewis told hundreds of fight fans gathered for the hall's induction ceremony. "I see it as a sweet science, a magical dance. For me, I just wanted to live up to that, and keep the dignity and the humanistic aspect and the positiveness of it…so that people will remember that's what I did for boxing." A towering presence at six feet, five inches and 250 pounds, the forty-three-year-old Lewis delivered these lines with the same degree of nimbleness he displayed in the ring—never before seen in a fighter his size. He entered the hall in his first year of eligibility with a record of 41-2-1, including thirty-two KOs.

"Boxing has taught me a lot in life—that dedication, discipline and determination will pay off in the long run and not to be easily swayed by obstacles and bumps in the road," Orlando Canizales said. Having left the ring in 1999, with a record of 50-5-1 with thirty-seven knockouts, the bantam was moved to tears as he accepted his enshrinement.

"It doesn't matter what the title is, or who you beat. It's not until you get this recognition from your peers that you know you have made it in boxing," Brian Mitchell said. Mitchell finished his career 45-1-3 with twenty-one KOs and is the first South African boxer to be enshrined in Canastota.

It will be these quotes that will be referenced in the future—as well they should—long after today's final bell. But the event itself will always be worth revisiting for the details, as there are so many stories between the ropes. Each new inductee redefines the induction criteria, be it ever so subtly—or in rare cases, significantly—applying another coat of varnish or removing another layer of tarnish from a sport that, at times, can be its own worst enemy.

For the returning members, they are the link to the past and a reminder of the importance of the sport to our history—timeless heroes who can still answer the bell. Along with the new inductees, they define the level of legitimacy to the institution. They are often carefully assembled just for this event. In 2001, the weekend boasted one of the finest collections of boxing trainers anywhere as George Benton, Gil Clancy, Angelo Dundee, Lou Duva, Eddie Futch and Emanuel Steward sat side by side. In 2002, eight opponents of Muhammad Ali were on hand: Chuvalo, Cooper, Norton, Terrell, Ellis, Shavers, Spinks and Lyle. A "Ring of Dreams" in Upstate New York—not Iowa!

For the special guests, rising stars and Parade of Champions grand marshals, attending the Induction Weekend is a rewarding experience. Since many of these individuals will never receive a plaque in Canastota, it is both a time to reunite with fans and to greet their own heroes.

The sign that greets you in the hall lobby reads, "Our mission is to honor and preserve boxing's rich heritage, chronicle the achievements of those who excelled and provide an educational experience for our many visitors." Mission accomplished!

A score has been settled. Canastota, New York, is "Title Town, USA."

BUFFALO'S GREAT LIGHTWEIGHT ERA

July 3, 1899–July 3, 1926

Frank Erne to Jimmy Goodrich to Rocky Kansas

KEY PARTICIPANTS

Frank Erne, 1891–1908; Harry Coulin, 1913–1921; Jake Schiffer, 1911–1921; Joey Mendo, 1915–1921; Lockport Jimmy Duffy, 1908–1921; Herman Smith, 1911–1922; Elmer Doane, 1913–1923; George Erne, 1910–1923; Kid Black, 1916–1923; Teddy Meyers, 1917–1924; Harry KO Mueller, 1918–1924; Jimmy Goodrich, 1918–1930; Rocky Kansas, 1911–1932

Selected entries

Selected Bibliography

BOOKS

Anderson, Dave. *In the Corner: Boxing's Greatest Trainers Talk about Their Art*. New York: William Morrow & Company, 1991.

Andre, Sam, and Nat Fleischer. *A Pictorial History of Boxing: From the Bare-Knuckle Days to the Present*. New York: Carol Publishing Group, 1981.

Baker, Mark Allen. *Complete Guide to Boxing Collectibles*. Iola, WI: Krause publications, 1995.

Bernstein, Peter L. *Wedding of the Waters*. New York: W.W. Norton & Co., 2005.

Boyd, Herb, with Ray Robinson II. *Pound for Pound: A Biography of Sugar Ray Robinson*. New York: Amistad, 2005.

Bromberg, Lester. *Boxing's Unforgettable Fights*. New York: Ronald Press, 1962.

Canastota-Oneida Area Italian American Committee, an Affiliate of the American Italian Heritage Association. *An American Journey—Our Italian Heritage: The Story of Immigrants and Their Descendants*. Canastota, NY: Canastota Publishing Company, 1998.

————. *An American Journey—Our Italian Heritage: The Story of Immigrants and Their Descendants*. Vol. II. Canastota, NY: Canastota Publishing Company, 2002.

Cassidy, Robert, Jr., and Steve Nicolaisen. *Boxing Legends of All Time*. With Mark Allen Baker, consultant. Lincolnwood, IL: Publications International, 1996.

Collins, Nigel. *Boxing Babylon Behind the Shadowy World of the Prize Ring*. New York: Carol Publishing Group, n.d.

Dundee, Angelo, with Bert Randolph Sugar. *My View from the Corner: A Life in Boxing*. New York: McGraw-Hill Books, 2008.

Dundee, Angelo, and Mike Winters. *I Only Talk Winning*. Chicago: Contemporary Books, 1985.

Finch, Roy G. *The Story of the New York State Canals*. N.p.: State of New York, 1925.

Fleischer, Nat. *50 Years at Ringside*. New York: Greenwood Press, 1969.

Goldstein, Ruby, and Frank Graham. *Third Man in the Ring*. Westport. CT: Greenwood Publishing Group, 1986.

Halberstam, David. *Summer of '49*. New York: Avon Books, Inc., 1989.

Heller, Peter. *In This Corner!* New York: Simon & Schuster, 1973.

Oates, Joyce Carol. *On Boxing*. Hopewell, NJ: The Ecco Press, 1994.

Robinson, Sugar Ray, and Dave Anderson. *Sugar Ray*. New York: Viking Press, 1970.

Sugar, Bert Randolph. *Bert Sugar on Boxing*. Guilford, CT: The Lyons Press, 2003.

———. *The 100 Greatest Boxers of All Time*. New York: Bonanza Books, 1964.

———. *One Hundred Years of Boxing: A Pictorial History of Modern Boxing, 1882–1982*. New York, 1982.

Weston. Stanley, and Steven Farhood. *The Ring: Chronicle of Boxing*. London: Hamlyn, 1993.

Whitford, Noble E. *History of the Canal System of the State of New York*. N.p., 1905.

INTERNET SOURCES

BoxRec.com, www.boxrec.com

Cyber Boxing Zone, www.cyberboxingzone.com

East Side Boxing, www.eastsideboxing.com

ESPN, msn.espn.go.com

International Boxing Hall of Fame, www.ibhof.com

International Boxing Research Association, www.ibroresearch.com

Library of Congress, Prints & Photographs Division, www.loc.gov

New York Times, www.nytimes.com

Sports Illustrated, www.si.com

Sweet Fights: www.sweetfights.com

Wikipedia, en.wikipedia.org

Articles, Associations and Related Materials

American Italian Heritage Association [Canastota-Oneida]

Bare Knuckle Boxing Hall of Fame, Belfast, NY

Bennett, Dick. "Backus Says Farewell to Fight Life." *Oneida Daily Dispatch*, July 28, 1978.

Buffalo Veteran Boxers Association, Ring #44, info@ring44.com

Canastota Bee-Journal. Boxing Showcase story. August 15, 1984, 24.

Central New York Regional Planning & Development Board

Greater Syracuse Sports Hall of Fame/Urban Sports Hall of Fame

Knowledge Systems & Research, Inc.

Rivest, Michael. "Quail Street Boxing: The City of Albany's Place to Train." *Albany Times Union.*

Rochester Boxing Hall of Fame

Sports Illustrated, February 25, 1957; September 16, 1957; March 24, 1958 [articles by Martin Kane].

Syracuse Herald-Journal. "Our Billy New Welterweight Champion." December 4, 1970. [Also a series of articles written by Tommy Ryan in 1911.]

Updike, John. "Hub Fans Bid Kid Adieu." *Assorted Prose*, 1965.

Historians

Jeff Brophy, Bob Collins, Herb Goldman, Don Hamilton, Hank Kaplan, Angelo Prospero, Paul Zabala and Buffalo Veteran Boxers Association, Ring #44 (e-mail: info@ring44.com; Jack Green, pres.; Jerry Collins, vice-pres.; Jim Brown, treas.; Angelo Prospero, hist.; Dick Wipperman, sgt. arms; Joe Cardenia, corr. sec.; and Bob Caico, rec. sec. Also, Bo Bilicki, Paul Wielopolski and Joe Mesi).

Reference Sources

Fleischer, Nat, Bert Sugar and Herbert G. Goldman et. al., eds. *The Ring Record Book & Boxing Encyclopedia*. 46 vols. N.p., 1941–1967.

Official Press Kit, 1995–2009. International Boxing Hall of Fame Induction, Canastota, NY. [Includes comprehensive and condensed biographies of inductees, plus numerous fact sheets and press releases.]

Roberts, James B., and Alexander G. Skutt. *The Boxing Register: International Boxing Hall of Fame Official Record Book*. 3rd ed. Ithaca, NY: McBooks Press, 2002.

MAGAZINES, NEWSPAPERS AND JOURNALS

Albany Times Union
Binghamton Press & Sun-Bulletin
Boston Globe
Boxing Illustrated
Buffalo Boxing Record
Buffalo News
Canastota Bee-Journal
Life
New York Daily News
New York Times
Ring
Rochester Democrat and Chronicle
Rochester Herald
South Buffalo News
Sport
SU Daily Orange
Syracuse Post-Standard
Utica Observer Dispatch

ADDITIONAL NOTES AND DISCLAIMERS

The *Ring* is published by London Publications and is the property of Golden Boy Enterprises subsidiary Sports and Entertainment Publications, LLC. The IBHOF logo is a trademark of the International Boxing Hall of Fame. Any additional logos or trademarks are property of their respective owners. Historic New York is part of the Education Department of the State of New York, Department of Public Works. Boxing sources vary; for example, some list Billy Backus's pro debut as September 16, 1961, against Ike Anthony. The information enclosed herein is provided without warranty of any kind either expressed or implied.

About the Author

Mark Allen Baker is a former business executive (General Electric/Genigraphics Corporation, assistant to the president and CEO), author (fifteen books), historian and writer (over two hundred articles). A graduate of the State University of New York, with postgraduate work completed at MIT, RIT and George Washington University, his expertise has been referenced in numerous periodicals, including *USA Today*, *Sports Illustrated* and *Money* magazine. Following his 1997 book, *Goldmine's Price Guide to Rock & Roll Memorabilia*, he appeared as a co-host on the VH-1 series *Rock Collectors*. Baker has also been a featured speaker at many events, including the Hemingway Days Festival and Writers Conference in Key West, Florida. He may also be familiar to some as the former co-owner of Bleachers Restaurant & Sports Bar (Liverpool, New York).

Acting as a historian for the International Boxing Hall of Fame, Baker is the only individual who has been a volunteer, chairperson and sponsor of an Induction Weekend event—both inside and outside the village of Canastota. He has also published artwork, articles and books related to the museum. Baker turns his attention to the hardwood for a book about basketball to be published in the fall of 2010.

He can be contacted at: PO Box 782, Hebron, CT, 06248.

Visit us at
www.historypress.net